The Challenge of Evil

Also by William Greenway
from Westminster John Knox Press

A Reasonable Belief: Why God and Faith Make Sense

The Challenge of Evil

Grace and the Problem of Suffering

WILLIAM GREENWAY

WESTMINSTER
JOHN KNOX PRESS
LOUISVILLE · KENTUCKY

First edition
Published by Westminster John Knox Press
Louisville, Kentucky

16 17 18 19 20 21 22 23 24 25—10 9 8 7 6 5 4 3 2 1

Book design by Sharon Adams
Cover design by Allison Taylor

Library of Congress Cataloging-in-Publication Data
Names: Greenway, William, 1963- author.
Title: The challenge of evil : grace and the problem of suffering / William
    Greenway.
Description: First edition. | Louisville, KY : Westminster John Knox Press,
    2016. | Includes index.
Identifiers: LCCN 2016032958 (print) | LCCN 2016036063 (ebook) | ISBN
    9780664262341 (pbk. : alk. paper) | ISBN 9781611647815 (ebook)
Subjects: LCSH: Suffering--Religious aspects--Christianity. | Good and
    evil--Religious aspects--Christianity. | Dostoyevsky, Fyodor, 1821-1881.
    Brat︠i︡a Karamazovy.
Classification: LCC BT732.7 .G739 2016 (print) | LCC BT732.7 (ebook) | DDC
    231/.8--dc23
LC record available at https://lccn.loc.gov/2016032958

Most Westminster John Knox Press books are available at special quantity discounts when purchased in bulk by corporations, organizations, and special-interest groups. For more information, please e-mail SpecialSales@wjkbooks.com.

For the Greenway-Leibowitz Family:
Tara, Larry, Dania Skye, and Elsa Larkin

The wisest men in every age have reached the same conclusion about life: *it's no good.*

—Nietzsche, *Twilight of the Idols*

. . . I absolutely renounce all higher harmony. It is not worth one little tear of even that one tormented child . . . . It's not that I don't accept God, Alyosha, I just most respectfully return him the ticket.

—Ivan Karamazov in Dostoevsky's *The Brothers Karamazov*

"That is my place in the sun." That is how the usurpation of the whole world began.

— Pascal, *Pensées*, as cited in Levinas, *Otherwise Than Being*

If we say that we have no sin, we deceive ourselves, and the truth is not in us. If we confess our sins, [God] who is faithful and just will forgive us our sins and cleanse us from all unrighteousness.

—1 John 1:8–9

". . . each of us is guilty in everything before everyone, and I most of all . . . verily each of us is guilty before everyone, for everyone and everything. . . ." Thus he awoke every day with more and more tenderness, rejoicing and all atremble with love . . . "Am I not in paradise now?"

—Markel Zosima in Dostoevsky, *The Brothers Karamazov*

Contents

Acknowledgments

First, I want to thank the many colleagues and students of Austin Presbyterian Theological Seminary who have, over the past two decades, been sources of wonderful conversation and insight. Second, I want to thank the wonderful people at Westminster John Knox Press, most especially my editor, Robert Ratcliff, and also Julie Tonini and Daniel Braden, for their superb editing; Allison Taylor, for design; and Emily Kiefer, for friendly publicity support. Third, back home in Austin, I owe sincere thanks to our redoubtable Executive Assistant to the Academic Dean, Alison Riemersma for, true to form, leaping into action to address some critical, time-sensitive challenges. Fourth, I once again owe my thanks to Professors Patrick Miller and John Leax, who provided me with absolutely essential encouragement as, amid a flurry of rejection letters for other projects, I pressed on with the writing of this book. Finally, I want to thank my mother, Sylvia Bailey Greenway, not only for her unconditional love and support, even when she could not quite bring herself to agree, but also for being one mean copyeditor!

Together with most anyone fortunate enough to have lived for more than half a century, I have known not only times of great joy but also times of fear, pain, grief, and loss. This book is focused on evil, pain, and suffering; so I want to acknowledge friends and in-laws, some now distant, who were sources of love and comfort amid times of personal fear, stress, and sorrow: Jamie and Darice Mullen, Carol Cook, Amy and Scott Black Johnston, Janet Parker, members of my old Koinonia class, and the amazing family I gained through marriage: Ethel, Chuck, Scott, Jasmine, Erika, Mark, Alice, and Oscar.

I am most thankful for those who fill my life and our home with joy day by day, for Cindy, Xander, Jessica, Kali, and Neville. This book is dedicated to my sister, Tara Greenway, and to her husband, Larry Leibowitz, who have also been sources of strength and comfort in hard times, and to their children, Dania Skye

Leibowitz and Elsa Larkin Leibowitz. I am so very thankful for their love and for the great Brooklyn style they bring into our lives. Finally, thanks to Larry's father, Marvin Leibowitz, and to his wife, Isa Leibowitz, who were concrete pillars of support and providers of joy for my parents and the rest of our family both during my father's illness and beyond.

William Greenway
Spring 2016
Austin, Texas

Introduction

The Spiritual Challenge of Evil

JOY EYES WIDE OPEN TO EVIL?

On the cover of *Thinking-of-the-Other*, a collection of essays by the celebrated philosopher Emmanuel Levinas (1906–1995), there appears a striking black-and-white photograph of the philosopher. The picture, obviously taken near the end of his long life, exudes an excess of energy. Elderly and vibrant, Levinas smiles at readers. Levinas's essays are deadly serious, but his eyes twinkle and his face glows with joy.[1]

How is this possible? Levinas's beloved younger brothers and parents—his entire immediate family—were murdered by the Nazi's *Schutzstaffel* (SS). His mother-in-law perished in the death camps. Levinas himself was a captive of the Nazis, isolated with fellow Jews in a Nazi labor camp from 1940–1945. While he almost never refers to the Holocaust explicitly, Levinas says his life work was "dominated by the presentiment and the memory of the Nazi horror."[2]

---

1. Emmanuel Levinas, *Entre Nous: Thinking-of-the-Other*, trans. Michael Smith and Barbara Harshav (New York: Columbia University Press, 1998).
2. Emmanuel Levinas, *Difficult Freedom: Essays on Judaism*, trans. Sean Hand (Baltimore: The Johns Hopkins University Press, 1997), 291.

Levinas was intimate witness to and victim of one of the most heinous evils in history. Thirty years later, nearly seventy years old, Levinas dedicated his most significant work, *Otherwise Than Being*, not only to "the memory of those who were closest among the six million assassinated by the National Socialists," and not only to all the other Jewish victims of the Holocaust, but also to "the millions on millions of all confessions and all nations, victims of the same hatred of the other man, the same anti-semitism."[3] Yet there he is on the cover of his book, no forgetfulness, no denial, no evasion, smiling, playful, joyful. How is that possible?

Of course, as Qoheleth (otherwise known as "The Teacher" or "The Quester") proclaims in Ecclesiastes, there is a time to mourn, a time to dance. But in that passage Qoheleth is speaking to the immediate reaction of individuals to daily events in life. We humans are discrete, spatially-temporally located journeys of awareness whose lived attention is always focused on some thought or thing or another, here and now on these words and their meaning, but in a moment, perhaps, on pangs of hunger, laughter from the next room, or the ding of a text or e-mail. On some days we celebrate birthdays, weddings, or successes. On other days we mourn illness, death, or failure. In the immediate moment, our reactions of joy or sorrow overflow with meaningfulness while remaining relatively nonreflective. That is, the immediate power of the meaningfulness of joyful or tragic daily events typically does not depend on the way they fit into some overall understanding of life. This can be especially true when the immediate event is especially joyous (the birth of one's beautiful baby) or searing (the death of that child in an automobile accident).

Levinas, however, is like Qoheleth: his sensitivities are not wholly consumed by the immediate. He is also vitally concerned with a vision of the whole. Like Qoheleth, when Levinas smiles out at us he bears in mind the whole panoply of joy, anguish, compassion, viciousness, delight, and suffering in our world. Bearing in mind a vision of the whole, Qoheleth says, yes, go ahead, laugh, dance, and celebrate, because there are times for that. But as for the whole, there is no pattern or purpose to be found. Every life is, ultimately, dust in the wind. "Vanity of vanities," Qoheleth concludes, "all is vanity" (Eccl. 12:8).

NIHILISM AND THE QUEST FOR MEANING

Notably, Levinas no more than Qoheleth believes in some eschatological day on which the righteous and wicked will receive their just desserts. Levinas, like Qoheleth, believes every life to be, ultimately, dust in the wind. Insofar as *appearances* are concerned, Levinas would affirm Qoheleth's nihilism, which has

---

3. Emmanuel Levinas, *Otherwise Than Being, or Beyond Essence*, trans. Alphonso Lingis (Pittsburgh: Duquesne University Press, 1981), v.

been resurgent in the modern West. Both could say, along with Shakespeare,
that

> Life's but a walking shadow, a poor player
> That struts and frets his hour upon the stage
> And then is heard no more: it is a tale
> Told by an idiot, full of sound and fury,
> Signifying nothing.[4]

In sum, while day by day our lives are infused with meaningfulness, times of joy
and times of mourning, once we lift our gaze from the immediate and consider
the whole, Qoheleth and Macbeth's nihilistic answer to the question of the
ultimate meaning of life can seem irrefutable.

As we will see, however, unlike Qoheleth and Macbeth, Levinas, in accord
with Jewish and Christian Scriptures, discerns a saving reality beyond the
appearances: namely, the reality of agape, the gracious love of God.[5] Nihilists,
in accord with predominant streams of modern Western rationality, dismiss the
idea that there is a saving spiritual reality beyond the appearances. They deny the
reality of divine love. At the same time, they attempt to protect us from despair
or even concern over the meaninglessness of the whole by concentrating our
attention on immediate realities.

Is it not the case, nihilists suggest, that the question of the ultimate meaning
of life is an abstraction, largely disconnected from our real, everyday lives and
concerns? Say there is no overarching meaning to the whole; could not awareness
of precisely that fact move us to treasure all the more passionately the rich panoply
of passion and meaning that fills our daily lives? Is Qoheleth not right, modern
nihilists say, to affirm that our day-to-day lives are pervaded with immediate
meaningfulness? Is there not, indeed, a time for every season under the sun, a
time for real, meaning-full, passionate dancing, and a time for real, meaning-
full, passionate mourning? Could there not be a certain dignity in consciously
and fully inhabiting the discrete panoply of meaningful moments that fill our
lives even as we remain fully aware that our existence is ultimately a fleeting
by-product of blind, purposeless processes? Would we not be truly foolish to be
so devastatingly dismayed and distracted by the ultimate meaninglessness of it
all that we disdain and miss out on the fleeting yet meaning-full-ness of all the
passion, sound, and fury suffusing daily life?

In the early twentieth century, the celebrated British philosopher Bertrand
Russell voiced just such a relatively hopeful nihilist vision. Russell concludes
that modern science confirms the bracing nihilism of Qoheleth and Macbeth.
Russell urges us to have the courage to face up to the brute character of existence.
Existence is incredibly complex, but it is ultimately a blind process with no

---

4. William Shakespeare, *Macbeth*, act V, scene 5.

5. I suspect Qoheleth/Ecclesiastes could be read as raising the pivotal existential/spiritual
question to which the balance of the Jewish and Christian Scriptures offer a saving response as they
unfold the reality of agape.

purpose, no direction, no memory, and no grand scheme. It is within this brute existence, says Russell, where, "if anywhere, our ideals henceforward must find a home":

> Man is the product of causes which had no prevision of the end they were achieving . . . his origin, his growth, his hopes and fears, his loves and his beliefs, are but the outcome of accidental collocations of atoms . . . all the labours of the ages, all the devotion, all the inspirations, all the noonday brightness of human genius, are destined to extinction in the vast death of the solar system . . . blind to good and evil, reckless of destruction, omnipotent matter rolls on its relentless way.[6]

Yet, Russell says, we need not and should not yield to despair, because what does remain for mortal "Man" is a saving possibility:

> to cherish, ere yet the blow falls, the lofty thoughts that ennoble his little day; disdaining the coward terrors of the slave of Fate, to worship at the shrine that his own hands have built; undismayed by the empire of chance, to preserve a mind free from the wanton tyranny that rules his outward life; proudly defiant of the irresistible forces that tolerate, for a moment, his knowledge and his condemnation, to sustain alone, a weary but unyielding Atlas, the world that his own ideals have fashioned despite the trampling march of unconscious power.[7]

In the same modern Western vein of heroic self-creation and defiant self-affirmation one might also cite—examples are legion—the secular epiphany of Russell's contemporary, the celebrated poet Wallace Stevens:

> The world about us would be desolate except for the world within us. The major poetic idea in the world is and always has been the idea of God. After one has abandoned a belief in God, poetry is the essence which takes its place as life's redemption.[8]

6. Bertrand Russell, "The Free Man's Worship," in *The Collected Papers of Bertrand Russell, vol. 12: Contemplation and Action, 1902–1914*, ed. Richard A. Rempel, Andrew Brink, and Margaret Moran (London: George Allen & Unwin, 1985), 71–72, as cited in E. A. Burtt, *The Metaphysical Foundations of Modern Science*, rev. ed. (Amherst, New York: Humanity Books, 1999), 23.

7. Russell, "Free Man's Worship," 72, as cited in Burtt, *Metaphysical Foundations*, 23. Astoundingly, in the midst of these concluding remarks Russell contends that because of a "tie of common doom, the free man finds that a new vision is with him always, shedding over every daily task the light of love" (71). The metaphysical source and character of this love, which I, following Levinas, account for, is manifest here as a felt necessity for Russell—but his philosophy cannot fund this appeal to love.

8. Wallace Stevens, *Opus Posthumous* (New York: Alfred A. Knopf, 1957), as cited in Charles Taylor, *Sources of the Self: The Making of the Modern Identity* (Cambridge: Harvard University Press, 1989), 493; Taylor references Stephen Spender, *The Struggle of the Modern* (Berkeley: University of California Press, 1963), 38–39, Spender cites Michael Hamburger, "Rilke among the Critics," *Encounter* 103 (April, 1962), 49–51. It is Hamburger who selects and groups these three discrete lines of prose from Wallace Stevens' *Opus Posthumous*.

NIHILISM AND THE SPIRITUAL CHALLENGE OF EVIL

The nihilism of Qoheleth, Macbeth, Russell, and Stevens is often considered to be bracingly honest, a resolute facing up to what we now know to be the hard, cold truth about reality. Again, insofar as *appearances* are concerned, Levinas would affirm nihilism. For Levinas and the balance of the Hebrew and Christian Scriptures, however, the appearances are deceptive. In truth, I will argue, inspired by Levinas and other Scriptures, nihilism denies the most significant dimension of reality and makes a devastating error when it abandons faith in God. To the faithful—I define "faith" below—to the faithful, the nihilist denial of God does not look bracingly honest. To the faithful, abandoning faith in God looks like an apologetic, protective move, if often unwitting, that allows modern Western nihilists to evade what would otherwise be humanity's most damning and devastating spiritual challenge: namely, the challenge of affirming ourselves and our world in the face of all the pain, suffering, and injustice suffusing existence. This is the spiritual challenge of evil—the challenge of affirmation in the face of evil.

Making clear how and why nihilism evades the spiritual challenge of evil is part of the task of part 1, "Modern Western Evasions of Evil." For ready evidence of the problem, however, note that *evil simply does not endure as a concern* for Qoheleth, Macbeth, Russell, or Stevens. If you do not evade the spiritual challenge of evil, then you realize the inadequacy of their responses as you consider that in the face of all the pain, suffering, and injustice one is not overcome by the vanity of it all. In the face of the pain, suffering, and injustice we are bludgeoned with conviction over the intense mattering of what is happening. The problem is not a lack of meaning, but the negativity of the meaning, the inability to affirm the meaningfulness by which we are seized as we scream out in anguish. Those who speak as if the ultimate challenge is meaningfulness itself, without addressing the meaningfulness of all the evil, without addressing the devastating accusation, evade the spiritual challenge of evil.

Notably, for those who do not evade the challenge, sensitivity to the spiritual challenge of evil can lie at the heart of one of the most powerful, passionate, and widespread reasons for rejecting faith in God: namely, outraged rejection of God in the wake of moral affront in this vale of tears. This is the rejection of God famously portrayed by Dostoevsky in the "Rebellion" chapter of *The Brothers Karamazov* (a focus of my closing chapters). In that chapter Ivan Karamazov, after recounting a litany of horrific (and historically true) events, proclaims that even one offense would be too much, that in his estimate even the tears of one child, let alone all the pain and suffering that pervades our world, would be too high a price to pay in order to purchase his own existence. Thus he suggests that, in the name of moral sensitivity to even the least degree of suffering, we should condemn the creator of this world.

Sensitivity to the spiritual challenge of evil is not the exclusive preserve of intellectual giants like Dostoevsky. When I explained to my mother how the spiritual challenge of evil and the moral objection to faith that flows from it was a prime focus of this study, she immediately responded, "it's everywhere." A few weeks earlier she had been chatting with a new neighbor in her retirement community in Florida. My mother mentioned her church. The woman responded with a story: When she was a child her fourteen-year-old brother had been hit by a car while riding his bike. He suffered severe brain trauma. For the next sixty years, she explained, he survived in a string of institutions. "I don't think a loving God would have allowed that to happen."

Insofar as this woman's rejection of God is empowered by moral passion it is admirable. Her moral passion should be affirmed with the utmost respect and her profound pain should be addressed with the highest pastoral sensitivity. Nonetheless, I will argue in chapter 1 that such an in a sense righteous rejection of God is self-contradictory and ultimately self-destructive, for it masks an unwitting evasion of the full force of evil's challenge to ultimate affirmation of ourselves, others, and the world. I will not attack the passion empowering such rejection or evade the spiritual challenge. *Any legitimate answer to the spiritual challenge of affirming ourselves, others, and the world in the face of evil will own and move through, not deny or evade, the moral passion that empowers such righteous rejection of God.* I strive to clarify the precise contours of such rejection of God, and I strive to unfold a way *through* our moral sensitivities *to* affirmation of reality, others, and ourselves, for the three-fold affirmation (i.e., of reality, others, and ourselves) and moments of pure joy are legitimate only if our eyes remain wide open to evil.

To be sure, there are times when the pain and suffering cut close, times of angst and tears. Our grief is undeniable and appropriate in such moments. I will in no way deny the reality of evil or the reality of times when grief, not joy, is appropriate. We should not feel joy when witnessing or remembering evil. There is indeed a time for mourning. In addition to daily news of war, crime, discrimination, illness, the plight of refugees, of impoverished peoples, the suffering of millions of creatures in factory farms—the awful litany goes on and on—science makes clear that our world is overwhelmingly and intractably burdened with pain, suffering, and violence. Over the course of history, innumerable creatures, including by far the vast majority of humans, have known disproportionate hardship, disappointment, sadness, and suffering.

Moreover, the spiritual challenge of affirmation does not rise up only in relation to times of pain, suffering, and injustice. The spiritual challenge of affirmation also arises in relation to times for joy in this vale of tears. Is there a legitimate time for pure joy? Should not joy always be chastened? Will not pure joy always depend on evasion, hard-heartedness, or denial? Can we be joyful even as our eyes remain wide open to all the evil suffusing reality? Must not a time for dancing depend on hard-heartedness about other, sorrow-drenched, wail-filled times and places?

It can surely seem self-evident that affirmation and pure joy require illegitimate suppressing of our deepest moral sensitivities. It can appear there is no honest way to affirm this world, others, and ourselves as primordially and ultimately good, given the depth and breadth of the world's suffering. Celebrated philosopher Charles Taylor says that denying evil in order to evade this devastating spiritual challenge was precisely why one of the most brilliant modern Western nihilists, Friedrich Nietzsche, argued that we should *overcome* our moral sensitivities. Taylor argues that acute moral sensitivity led Nietzsche to conclude that since our moral ideals cannot be met after faith in God is abandoned, they must be overcome. Realizing the depth of conviction permeating modern Westerners' most widely shared moral sensitivities, Nietzsche speaks of a *self*-overcoming of moral sensitivities, a self-overcoming that allows one to affirm the world "even though it remains the domain of blind, unspiritual, chaotic forces."[9] As Taylor explains, Nietzsche believes that

> Morality brought us to the notion of something pure and great and infinitely worth affirmation and love—only it wasn't us as we are, but the negation of our essential being, the denial of the will to power. What we have to do . . . is overcome the force of morality and find the strength to rise above its demands, which sap our strength and fill us with the poison of self-hatred . . . . This power to affirm does indeed repose in us . . . what really commands affirmation is this very power itself . . . . We can say "yes" to all that is.[10]

Those who overcome the moral can affirm world and self, but now what is affirmed is a sort of beauty that arises not in the world itself, but in our power to say yes to all that is, in our power to adopt a "stance of unflinching acceptance."[11] Because of the pain, suffering, and injustice suffusing the world, this affirmation, this "yes," can only be uttered if I have moved beyond good and evil, if I have overcome my moral sensitivities. According to Nietzsche, if we can overcome our conditioning to think and feel morally, if we can move beyond every last vestige of thinking and feeling in terms of good and evil, then we will be freed from losing ourselves to any sense of good and evil, then we will escape any sense of guilt or judgment, then we can glory in our capacity to look, judge, and act in accord with what we decide to enjoy and prefer.

For Nietzsche, then, nihilism facilitates a sort of salvation. Nihilism involves the rejection of moral reality. Since the universe is without meaning and purpose, we can abandon ideas of right and wrong (and our sensibilities about them). This rejection of morality is salvific because it frees us from our moral sensitivities and the condemnation they bring in this vale of tears. Thereby, nihilism wholly undercuts the basis of the devastating spiritual challenge of affirmation in the face of evil. This can sound liberating. However, Taylor warns, we sacrifice mightily for this liberation, because Nietzschean self-overcoming requires us to excise our moral sensitivities. Indeed, because it involves destruction of our own

9. Taylor, *Sources*, 453.
10. Ibid.
11. Ibid., 454.

most profound and sure moral sensitivities, Taylor deems this rejection of moral reality to be a sort of spiritual mutilation.[12]

Taylor defends moral realism (i.e., the idea that good and evil are real, not simply contingent products of evolutionary psychological and sociological dynamics), but at the same time he sees affirmation of moral realism as an awesome threat, for our moral ideals stand in devastating contrast to the harsh realities of existence and, unfortunately, many of our own thoughts and actions. The tension between our moral sensitivities and extant reality turns our desire to affirm the moral meaningfulness of life, including the desire to affirm ourselves as good, into a dilemma of mutilation. For when we acknowledge our most profound and sure moral sensitivities they turn in our hands and, in the glare of our own and our world's imperfection and cruelty, preclude us from affirming either the world or ourselves (thus, says Taylor, Nietzsche believes moral demands "sap our strength and fill us with the poison of self-hatred").[13] Our very understandings of right and wrong justifiably accuse us of complicity in the world's suffering. We appear to face a harsh either-or: *either* we affirm our moral sensitivities and condemn ourselves and our world, *or* we excise our moral sensitivities and liberate ourselves from condemnation, but at the cost of spiritual mutilation.

Taylor calls this either-or the West's "greatest spiritual challenge."[14] He remains unsure how we might meet it, but he refuses to accept it as an iron fate.[15] He says that while he cannot yet explain how we might escape this devastating either-or, he suspects the answer lies in the sort of hope he sees, "implicit in Judeo-Christian theism (however terrible the record of its adherents in history), and in its *central promise of a divine affirmation of the human, more total than humans can ever attain unaided.*"[16]

Taylor does not know how to unfold or justify this hope in divine affirmation, but he thinks Fyodor Dostoevsky, most especially in his classic, final work, *The Brothers Karamazov*, identifies two essential elements. First, individuals must accept themselves as responsible subjects. Second, "a central idea of the Christian tradition," people must be "transformed through being loved by God, a love that they mediate to each other."[17] Taylor does not develop these spiritual overtures in *Sources of the Self*, and while he has produced significant works in the intervening quarter century, he nowhere develops this gesture toward an answer to the spiritual challenge of affirmation of ourselves, of others, and of the world in the face of evil.[18]

12. Ibid., 520.
13. Ibid., 453.
14. Ibid.
15. Ibid.
16. Ibid., emphasis mine.
17. Ibid., 452.
18. Charles Taylor, *Philosophical Arguments* (Boston: Harvard University Press, 1997); *The Ethics of Authenticity* (Boston: Harvard University Press, 1992); *A Secular Age* (Boston: Harvard University Press, 2007); Hubert Dreyfus and Charles Taylor, *Retrieving Realism* (Boston: Harvard

Taking up where Taylor leaves off, I strive to unfold the reality of a divine affirmation of all creatures and to explain how this divine "yes" meets the spiritual challenge of affirmation even as we squarely face evil. I strive to affirm the truth and significance of agape. I will be unveiling the character and reality of agape in detail throughout this reflection. In short, agape is gracious love that we receive for all others and for ourselves: that is, agape is not *from* me; it is a gift *received* for all (including me). Agape is the saving reality at the heart of Christian spirituality and, insofar as one follows Levinas, agape is the saving reality at the heart of Jewish spirituality (and, I would expect, the saving reality at the heart of diverse faith/wisdom traditions). More precisely, I strive to explain how the reality of agape allows us to move through the spiritual challenge of affirmation in the face of evil by gifting us with a primordial and ultimate affirmation of reality, others, and ourselves—and even legitimating moments of pure joy.[19]

In all of this, note well, I am addressing and clarifying the intimate relationship between two familiar challenges in modern Western thought: the challenge of *the quest for meaning* and the challenge of the *problem of evil*. Just above, I began by tracing the essential challenge of the quest for meaning as it has arisen in the wake of facing up to an influential, atheistic, modern Western naturalistic picture of reality (also known as the physicalist, materialist, naturalistic, or scientistic picture of reality). As illustrated in Nietzsche, Russell, and Stevens, for materialists the quest for meaning turns into a quest to learn to accept our finitude, a quest to abandon pretensions to eternal or God-ensured, supra-historical meaningfulness, a quest to learn how fully to affirm and rejoice in the finite but meaning-full character of day to day life.

As Taylor's unfolding of the dilemma of mutilation makes clear, however, given the pain, suffering, and injustice suffusing reality, insofar as the quest for meaning is simultaneously a quest for affirmation, the quest for meaning runs up against the *spiritual* challenge of evil (in contrast, for example, to running up against evil as a *logical* challenge for those arguing for the existence of God, or as a *practical* challenge in relation to concrete evils we should struggle against).

University Press, 2015). Clearly still convinced about the significance of faith, Taylor refers to faith in the closing sentence of his most recent book (*Retrieving Realism*, 2015), but in that book Dreyfus and Taylor's discussion of the significance of faith for philosophical spirituality is far more marginal than is Taylor's discussion in *Sources of the Self*, and the possible role of faith is far more cryptic in *Retrieving Realism* than it is in relation to the clear, if undeveloped, reference to hope in divine affirmation in the closing paragraph of *Sources*. More troubling for those of us concerned over ethical disregard for and human exploitation of other creatures, Dreyfus and Taylor overtly link retrieval of moral and religious realism with "distinguishing our way of being from that of the animals" (*Retrieving Realism*, 166). Notably, many philosophers pilloried Taylor for his serious references to God in *Sources*. For an account of this widespread, hostile reaction, and a defense of the perspicuity of Taylor's framing of the dilemma of mutilation, see my essay, "Charles Taylor on Affirmation, Mutilation, and Theism: A Retrospective Reading of *Sources of the Self*," *Journal of Religion* 80 (January 2000): 23–40.

19. In very technical terms, I will argue that Levinasian "substitution" delineates the essence of an essentially (but not exclusively) Christian understanding of the dynamics of expiation: namely, how "faith in God"/"awakening to agape," without any evasion or denial of evil, delivers spiritual salvation.

The quest for meaning runs up against the spiritual challenge of affirmation in the face of evil because, in light of all the evil permeating our world and ourselves, the ultimate word on our world and ourselves is not the relatively benign "we are all dust in the wind," which designates us as finite but innocent, but the conclusion Nietzsche is so desperate to escape: "The wisest men in every age have reached the same conclusion about life: *it's no good.*"[20] In the light of this judgment, it becomes clear that not only Nietzsche's, but also Russell and Stevens' nihilistic affirmations of meaning depend on denial of moral reality, that is, on spiritual mutilation, for their nihilistic affirmations depend on an overcoming—intentional or unwitting—of our most profound and sure moral sensitivities.

In this book, inspired especially by Jewish philosopher Emmanuel Levinas and Christian novelist Fyodor Dostoevsky, I strive to meet the spiritual challenge of affirmation in the face of evil by explaining how the reality of agape at the heart of Jewish and Christian faith (and, I expect, at the heart of other faiths) gifts us with a primordial and ultimate spiritual affirmation of our world, of others, and of ourselves, and even legitimates moments of pure joy, all without denial or evasion, eyes wide open to all the pain, suffering, and injustice suffusing reality.[21] Moreover, beyond the level of explanation and reason, I strive to awaken readers to agape, or to strengthen and affirm those readers already awakened to agape, and thereby to stimulate and affirm our joy and primordial and ultimate affirmation of the world, of others, and of ourselves—even as we keep our eyes wide open to enduring evil.

ON PHILOSOPHICAL SPIRITUALITY

A human author can only speak from within the conceptual contours of one cultural and religious tradition or another (including secular humanist and other atheist traditions). I speak as a modern Western Christian theologian and philosopher formed by the Christian and Jewish traditions. On the other hand, acknowledgment of contextual specificity does not entail affirmation of conceptual relativity or warrant irrational appeals. This exploration remains wholly within the bounds of what is considered to be reasonable and good according to common public standards. Working within these bounds, some beliefs and forms of understanding can clearly be affirmed with more surety (if not "certainty") than others—and many beliefs and forms of understanding deservedly enjoy global authority.

20. Friedrich Nietzsche, *The Anti-Christ, Ecce Homo, Twilight of the Idols, and Other Writings,* trans. A. Judith Norman, ed. Aaron Ridley (Cambridge: Cambridge University Press, 2005), 162.
21. In more traditional theological language: I will be unfolding the dynamic that Christians testify to wonderingly in terms of finding themselves saved by faith, the gift of grace, even as they wholly own and confess their complicity and culpability—*simul iustus et peccator* (i.e., simultaneously redeemed and convicted), says Luther.

In particular, I do not countenance any "leaps of faith" or presume from the start the truth of any particular tradition, creed, scripture, or religious authority. I limit my explorations to what theologians call "general revelation" (awakening to the divine available to any and all who open their hearts and minds) in contrast to "special revelation" (knowledge directly conveyed by a deity). I neither affirm nor contest the reality of special revelation. I neither affirm nor contest the truth of beliefs insofar as they depend on special revelation. Making no judgments about special revelation, I strictly delimit this exploration of faith to the bounds of what is reasonable and good according to common public standards. Thus delimited, this work constitutes a *philosophical spirituality*.

Insofar as diverse cultures and faith traditions are truly dealing with a transcending reality, it is most reasonable to expect all faiths to have been inspired by the same transcending reality. As a Christian, I cannot speak definitively for other faith traditions, but I suspect the essence of Christian spirituality is continuous with the essential spirituality of Jewish, Islamic, Hindu, Buddhist, and many other faith/wisdom traditions. If so, then I would expect this specifically (but not exclusively) Christian and Jewish (insofar as I follow Levinas) explanation of the way in which faith facilitates affirmation without evasion of evil to be in accord with the dynamics of affirmation in other faith traditions—indeed, affirmation of analogous dynamics in other faith traditions (insofar as they are reasonable) would confirm surety about this explanation, while objections (again, insofar as they are reasonable) would alert us to potential confusions.[22]

KEY TERMS

For the sake of clarity, let me briefly define some key terms.[23] First, I will explain what I mean by two unusual but critically important terms that I draw from Levinas: namely, "awakening" and "Face" (in contrast to lowercased "face," I will capitalize "Face" when using it in a technical, Levinasian sense). Then I will explain what I mean by four other key terms: namely, "agape," "faith," "good," and "evil." Finally, I will explain what I mean by the most audacious term of all, "God" (or, to use the more reverent Jewish spelling, "G-d"), the term that

22. In order to protect against the introduction of background concepts dependent on special revelation or on unsupported appeals to tradition, I will be largely avoiding classical theological terms. To be sure, however, when I speak of the possibility of affirmation of ourselves and others without evasion of evil, all in relation to surrender to having been seized in and by love, I understand myself to be attempting to unfold and gesture toward the essential meaning of what in classical Christian theological terms would be discussed in terms of confession of sin, forgiveness of sins, and salvation from sin that we receive through the gift of God's grace.

23. I unfold and defend my understanding of these terms at length in William Greenway, *A Reasonable Belief: Why God and Faith Make Sense* (Louisville, KY: Westminster John Knox Press, 2015). While there are small differences in formulation, the essential definition of key terms and my methodology (i.e., the role of reason in this philosophical spirituality) remain the same as in *A Reasonable Belief.*

signifies an Other whose ways transcend our ways (Isa. 55:8–9), whom we now see only "in a mirror, dimly" (1 Cor. 13:12), and whose peace "surpasses all understanding" (Phil. 4:7).

Let me begin with my appropriation of Levinas's concept of Face, and let me start with a sobering, concrete example. A couple of weeks ago, on Memorial Day weekend, the Blanco River rose twenty-six feet in one hour and ravaged the small town of Wimberley, Texas (about sixty miles southwest of Austin). The torrent uprooted massive, one-hundred-year-old trees and destroyed hundreds of homes. One mother and her two young children were in Wimberley for the weekend. In the middle of the stormy night their house, built on thick concrete stilts meant to elevate the home out of harm's way, was swept off its foundations. The house remained largely intact as it began to float down the swollen river. The mother was able to reach her sister by cell phone. In a brief conversation she explained to her sister that they were trapped in the house and floating down the river. She told her sister how much she loved her and told her to tell their parents how much she loved and was thankful for them. A few minutes later the river rammed the house into a bridge, tearing it to pieces, and throwing everyone into the debris-filled torrent. As I write, the bodies of the mother and children have yet to be found.[24]

That horrific, unthinkable event can be accurately described in terms of appearances, that is, in terms of biology, sociology, hydrology, psychology, and other of the natural or social sciences. While such scientific descriptions of the reality are accurate and very important, they are not only incomplete but also unable to discern the most profound dimensions of the event, the terror and the significance of the end of those precious faces. When we are *awakened* (in the sense of the term that I am here proposing) to this story, it is not because we consciously choose to care for those people or because we deliberately desire the horror and sorrow the story awakens in us. Rather, insofar as we are awakened, insofar as we encounter not only *faces* (the physical and historical facts of their lives) but also *Faces* (their infinite worth), we are seized by concern, horror, and sorrow. In other words, we are not awakened to Faces because we choose to be but because we find ourselves grasped—in ways that transcend understanding— by their irreducible, infinite value. Because of the involuntary way in which we are seized by Faces, Levinas, who had ample like experiences during his five years of captivity in a Nazi forced labor camp, speaks of how we are *taken hostage* by the Faces of others.

To explain Levinas's point in more abstract terms, lowercase "face" refers to faces in the ordinary sense (e.g., eyes, skin, nose). When I speak of uppercase Face in Levinas's technical sense, by contrast, I am not naming anything about the physical appearance of a face; I am speaking of the way in which I am *taken hostage by* that face. To speak of having been taken hostage by a face is to speak

---

24. I am not using names out of respect. Many others in Wimberley and along the Blanco River were killed or grievously wounded by the flood.

of the Face of the face. The Face, in contrast to the face, is not a biological or sociocultural reality. Gender, ethnicity, height, age, and so forth are all features of one's face. Following Levinas, however, the Face of any face refers to the way I find myself not only discerning the features of a face, as I may discern the features of a house or car, but to the way in which Faces, for instance, the Faces of that mother and her children, take me hostage. The capitol "F" designates this dimension of reality—in this sense even creatures without faces have Faces.

Levinas concedes we can choose to shut ourselves off from Faces.[25] We can harden our hearts. In this respect Levinas's "hostage" metaphor is less than helpful, for hostages are not free to reject being hostages. So instead of saying "taken hostage" I will say, "having been seized." Moreover, I want to make explicit two points that remain implicit in Levinas. First, I am seized by *passionate concern for* others. Since this is a passionate concern that *is not from me but is my passionate concern for others*, this amounts to saying that I am seized by *agape*. Second, insofar as this passionate concern does not originate in me but is an enveloping reality to which I have been awakened in the event of having been seized by love for others, I realize *agape* is a real dimension of the ultimate reality *in which I live and move and have my being*. In order to make all three of these emphases explicit—potential to harden heart, *by agape, in agape*—where Levinas would say, "taken hostage by the face," I will say, *having been seized in and by love for Faces*. So, I would say that as we hear the awful story of that mother and her two children, we find ourselves having been seized in and by love for their Faces, and so we are horrified, we mourn them, and our hearts ache for their friends and family.

While it is vital and accurate to recognize the passive character of having been seized in and by love, the ability to harden one's heart is vital, for it preserves the integrity of my free will and thereby my authentic, freely self-created identity. Let me reiterate and stress a vital characteristic in the dynamic. Namely, while I can choose to harden my heart, I cannot choose to be seized by others' Faces, for having been seized in and by love precedes any thought, intention, or decision on my part. Because I can harden my heart, however, when I do not harden my heart to having been seized in and by love, my love for Faces is authentically mine even though it does not originate in me. I will call not hardening one's heart "surrender," but it is vital to remember that "surrender" in this context is not an action, rather, it is *not taking* an action, *not* hardening one's heart to having been seized in and by love.[26]

We often find ourselves most dramatically seized in moments of crisis, but the context may also be wonderful. Perhaps I am walking by a church and I see joyful, laughing newlyweds running out to the limo beneath a light rain of birdseed and suddenly I find myself happy and smiling. I have been seized by

25. In Levinas' words, "if no one is good voluntarily [i.e., good does not originate in I's free will], no one is enslaved to the Good" (Levinas, *Otherwise than Being*, 11).

26. This is the sense in which, in Christian theology, grace is neither a work nor a negation of our autonomy and authentic loving.

the Faces of those newlyweds. Levinas claims Faces beckon even when I pass strangers on the street. Even then, those who are awakened find themselves called to say hello. Levinas is not suggesting we walk the streets of Manhattan saying hello to everyone. The awakened, however, feel the call of every Face even in Manhattan, where, sensitive to context, they are hopefully wise enough to know when to suppress any urge to make eye contact.

The relationship among Faces may not be reciprocal. For instance, I may find myself seized by the Face of an infant who is as of yet incapable of seeing and being seized by concern for my Face. The Face may also be manifest and not reciprocated in creatures we do not ordinarily think of as having Faces. Imagine you have come to my lecture and I walk in and give everyone a brittle stick gathered from the parking lot. I ask people to break the sticks into pieces. I get odd looks, but people typically break the sticks in order to humor me.

Now, imagine I walk you outside to a very young tree, say a foot-high maple sapling. The sapling is in a splendid location, not in the way of anything, and I hand you a hoe and say (at some cost, even in the imagining), "Tear it out of the ground by the roots so that it cannot possibly recover." Usually, people visibly recoil when they hear this request. Even with regard to a sapling, many look up with expressions of horror. They have been seized in and by love for the Face of the sapling.[27] Notably, the Face of the sapling, like all Faces, *is manifest solely and precisely in awakening to having been seized in and by love for its Face.* Indeed, manifestation of Faces is simultaneous with manifestation of agape. Insofar as we are awake, from saplings to humans, our world shimmers with a sea of glorious Faces.

27. The *ethical* violation involved in the killing of a sapling (perhaps a human needs it for heat or shelter) would not be equivalent to the ethical violation involved in the killing of a human. This raises the properly ethical question of how to adjudicate among the violations of the Faces of various faces. Such questions remain beyond the scope of this work because I am focused on awakening to moral violation wherever any life, even the life of a sapling, is destroyed (see William Greenway, "Peter Singer, Emmanuel Levinas, Christian Agape, and the Spiritual Heart of Animal Liberation," *Journal of Animal Ethics*, 5:2 [Fall 2015]: 167–80). I should note that Levinas, still confined by modern Western anthropocentrism, did not extend his category of "Face" beyond the human species. The exclusion, while contextually unsurprising, is unjustifiable. Levinas may have indicated some potential for openness on this issue when he said that he does not know whether or not a snake has a face and explicitly affirmed that the ethical (i.e., our ethical responsibility) "extends to all living beings"—though he immediately stresses that only "the human breaks with pure being" ("The Paradox of Morality: An Interview with Emmanuel Levinas," trans. Andrew Benjamin and Tamra Wright, in *The Provocation of Levinas: Rethinking the Other*, ed. Robert Bernasconi and David Wood [London: Routledge, 1988], 171–72). For those familiar with Levinas, the story of the welcoming dog, Bobby, whom Levinas encountered in captivity, speaks even more profoundly to this issue (and suggests that it is not only the human that breaks with pure being): Levinas credits Bobby with seeing Levinas's Face, and in this sense delivering to Levinas Levinas's own Face when its reality was being so violently denied by other humans. This goes beyond saying that Bobby has a Face because Levinas, to a degree, receives his own Face when he sees Bobby seeing his (i.e., Levinas's) Face. That is, Bobby not only has a Face, Bobby *sees* Faces. So, in a way that no doubt transcends Bobby's understanding, Bobby is awakened (Emmanuel Levinas, *Is It Righteous to Be? Interviews with Emmanuel Levinas*, ed. Jill Robbins [Stanford: Stanford University Press, 2001], 90, and Emmanuel Levinas, "The Name of a Dog, or Natural Rights," *Difficult Freedom*, 151–53).

In short, *agape* beneath, behind, and around one is unveiled in having been seized in and by love for the Faces of others. The question for freely self-creating I's in the face of having been seized in and by love is whether or not they will harden their hearts. I's who do not harden their hearts, that is, I's *who live surrender to (release themselves to) having been seized in and by love, are I's of faith. Faith is living surrender to agape.*

Faith, then, is not something I create, assert, or intend. Faith is not knowledge I have or my assent to some set of beliefs. Beliefs are significant insofar as they are ideas we have about faith and allow for testimony and shared understanding. A system of beliefs about faith constitutes a faith tradition. Intellectual assent to even the most wonderful and full system of beliefs, however, is not faith. Faith is continually living surrender to having been seized in and by love for all Faces, continually living surrender to the surpassing reality of agape in which we live and move and have our spiritual being. In living surrender to agape, we are faithful. In our continual living surrender to having been seized in and by love, we freely receive faith, the gift of agape.

This understanding of Faces, agape, and faith allows for precise definition of the ethical meaning of "good" and "evil." In brief, the primordial moral reality is agape, the love for all Faces in and by which we are seized. "Good" and "evil" in the ethical sense (in contrast, most notably, to "good" and "bad" in an aesthetic sense) names the relationship among events or actions, Faces, and agape. Insofar as an event or action violates a Face, it is evil. Insofar as an event or action enhances or brings joy to a Face, it is good.

Both natural events and deliberate actions can be good or evil. For instance, whether a Face is harmed by cancer, flood, or tornado (i.e., natural events), or is harmed deliberately by another person (i.e., an intentional action), the violation of that Face is evil. Notably, neither the cancer nor the hurtful person is intrinsically evil. In the case of the person (or any agent, in accord with capacity) one would also invoke categories of ethical character and culpability (e.g., what Judaism and Christianity speak of in terms of sin and sinfulness). Such categories do not apply to cancer, floods, or tornados (tornados never sin).

Finally, let me give some initial sense for the meaning of the most audacious term of all: namely, the meaning of "God" in the context of this exploration—and let me reiterate that my reflections here are strictly delimited by the boundaries of general revelation. I mean "God" insofar as "God is love." When I speak of *faith in God*, then, I am not referring to a set of *beliefs about God*, I am speaking of not hardening my heart *to* having been seized in and by *love*.[28] That is, when in this context I speak of faith in God I am speaking of living surrender to agape, living surrender to God.

To be sure, "God" in this delimited sense does not include all the characteristics of the personal or triune God who is the classic subject of Jewish or Christian

---

28. Because I could harden my heart to faith, when I do not harden my heart the faith is mine without my autonomy being violated. As the same time, the faith is not my doing/work.

faith. Again, what "God" can mean within the bounds of this philosophical spirituality is delimited by the boundaries of *general* revelation (it remains within the bounds of reason). This delimitation does not entail rejection of special revelation or of a personal or triune God. Not only does nothing here contradict belief that God is personal or triune, but these reflections may also be a sure step on the way to more particular and complete confessions of faith in God. Proclamation that "God is love/agape," moreover, is a classic and essential aspect of Jewish, Christian, and many other confessions of faith. Select lines from 1 John 4 proclaim the essence of what I mean when I speak of "God" within the parameters of this philosophical spirituality:

> Beloved, let us love one another, because love is from God; everyone who loves is born of God and knows God. Whoever does not love does not know God, for God is love. . . . In this is love, not that we loved God but that [God] loved us . . . God is love, and those who abide in love abide in God, and God abides in them (1 John 4:7–8, 10a, 16b).

AFFIRMATION WITHOUT EXPLAINING/ JUSTIFYING EVIL (I.E., WITHOUT THEODICY)

In order to forestall what would be an understandable confusion, let me clarify that I will *not* offer some ultimate explanation of, or justification for, evil. I will not offer a philosophical explanation of why—considering the whole of existence, or with reference to multiple possible worlds, or putting pain, suffering, and injustice into balance with goods that flow from pain, suffering, and injustice—I will not offer a philosophical explanation of why we can affirm existence on the whole because, on balance, evil serves a greater good. Nor will I offer a theological explanation as to why, with reference to God and life after death, we can understand evil as on balance something that on the whole works together for the good. Some such philosophical or theological explanation may exist, but to date no explanation or theodicy has come close to gaining general acceptance.

If I were developing an argument for the existence of God in the standard modern Western fashion, then my failure to develop a theodicy—which is to say in standard form, my inability to explain how and/or why, if there is an omnipotent, perfectly good God, there is also evil—would be a major problem. Notably, none of the classic texts or major theologians in any of the world's faith traditions has ever proceeded by developing proofs for the existence of the divine (i.e., none of the world's wisdom traditions equate faith with the conclusion of an argument). Accordingly, while the faith in God I defend is, given generally accepted modern Western standards of what is reasonable and good, wholly reasonable, it is not the conclusion of an argument.

I do not reject the standard, *logical*, modern Western "problem of evil," nor do I dismiss the possibility of an explanation/theodicy. If there is a God who has the agency required to prevent some or all of the evils in the world, then that God does indeed have some explaining to do. If there is such a God, then, in accord with a logic and perspective I currently find unimaginable, there may well be an explanation/justification for all the evil and, divinely enlightened, I might find that explanation understandable. But at present I cannot imagine any such explanation, and no philosophical or theological attempt to provide any such explanation has come close to gaining general acceptance.

Moreover, I join Levinas when, remembering smoke from concentration camp ovens, he insists on the category of useless suffering.[29] That is, my unfolding of a primordial and ultimate, three-fold spiritual affirmation of world, others, and ourselves will endure even as we acknowledge the moments, minutes, and possibly years when we have been, are, or may yet be wholly consumed by horror. And the three-fold affirmation will endure even as we acknowledge the very real possibility that we ourselves may be wholly obliterated by horror— murdered, unjustly and utterly gone forevermore, period.

In sum, I will not offer an explanation for evil. I will not develop a theodicy. I will not finish with a coherent, ribbon-tied vision of the whole. I will not offer a magic pill that can protect us from evil, prevent our anguish, or magically take away our sorrow. I will insist on the category of useless suffering. Above all, however, I will strive to unfold how, squarely facing evil, eyes wide open to enduring evil, wholly aware that we could be literally and utterly consumed by evil, we nonetheless can wholly reasonably be awakened to primordial and ultimate affirmation of reality, of others, and of ourselves, and on occasion can fully inhabit moments of pure joy.

I unfold an argument in accord with generally accepted standards for what is reasonable and good. My goal, however, is not to prove the truth of a proposition affirmed/known/grasped (e.g., "God exists"). My aim is reasoned *awakening* to a reality: namely, reasoned awakening to a love in and by which, insofar as we have not hardened our hearts, we find ourselves always already seized, and the unfolding of an explanation as to how that reality, eyes wide open to evil, delivers primordial and ultimate affirmation of the world, others, and ourselves, and even legitimates (i.e., no evasion, no denial) moments of pure joy. In other words, as a Christian theologian inspired above all by the Jewish philosopher Emmanuel Levinas, I strive to stimulate awakening to divine reality and to make clear how faith in God, that is, how living surrender to having been seized in and by love, delivers affirmation and joy even as our eyes remain wide open to evil.[30]

---

29. Levinas, "Useless Suffering," in *Entre Nous*, 91–101.

30. This book focuses on the spiritual challenge of evil. In *A Reasonable Belief*, I focus more broadly on unfolding the reasonableness of faith. As is clear in *A Reasonable Belief*, I am especially indebted not only to Emmanuel Levinas, but also to the Catholic theologian, Jean-Luc Marion, most particularly to his essay, "Sketch of a Phenomenological Concept of Gift," in *Postmodern Philosophy and Christian Thought*, ed. Merold Westphal (Bloomington: Indiana University Press, 1999), 122–43. In a sister volume, *For the Love of All Creatures: The Story of Grace in Genesis* (Grand Rapids, MI: William B. Eerdmans Publishing Company, 2015), I unfold this same spirituality in conversation with the *Enuma Elish*, the *Gilgamesh Epic*, and above all with Hebrew Scripture, primarily the primeval history of

THE ARGUMENT

The argument unfolds in three parts. In part 1, "Modern Western Evasions of Evil," I consider three influential modern Western conceptual trajectories that evade the spiritual challenge of evil. In chapter 1, "Unwitting Evasion: Suffering and Righteous Rejection of God," I am sympathetic to and even admiring of passionate and in a sense righteous rejection of God in the face of suffering, but I explain why this indignant rejection of God is self-contradictory and ultimately self-destructive, for it masks an unwitting evasion of the full force of evil's challenge to spiritual affirmation.

In chapter 2, "Salvation after the Death of God: Nietzsche," I expand the dialogue with Nietzsche begun in this introduction (and, through him, with modern Western nihilism generally) and provide a detailed and, inasmuch as is possible, sympathetic response to his devastating suggestion that we secure affirmation by self-overcoming our most profound and sure moral sensitivities.

In chapter 3, "Biocentrism and Faces: Deep Ecology and the Land Ethic," and chapter 4, "Aldo Leopold and the Wolf: A Confession Betrayed," I respond to two closely related and influential modern Western "green" spiritualities, deep ecology (Arne Naess) and the land ethic (Aldo Leopold), both of which are commonly characterized as biocentric (in the sense of life or earth-centered). The spirituality of biocentrism will be familiar to anyone who has found solace, joy, and a sense of communion and peace in mountain vistas, ocean depths, or solitary hikes through alpine meadows. Judaism and Christianity, along with most all other faiths, celebrate spiritual experiences mediated through such surpassing glory in creation. Unsurprisingly, since I am a Christian inspired by the Jewish philosopher Emmanuel Levinas, my response to Naess and Leopold will be sympathetic and affirming. In the end, however, I will argue that affirmation of biocentric spirituality must be carefully qualified, for biocentrism subtly evades the spiritual challenge of evil insofar as it fails to value individuals.

In part 2, "Agape and the Paradise of 'Yes,'" I explain how faith delivers salvation without evasion, for faith is surrender to the reality of agape, that is, surrender to a gracious, primordial, ultimate, always already present "yes" to existence, others, and ourselves. I will explain why, far from pain, suffering, and injustice being realities we must forget, deny, or evade in order to be joyful, legitimate joy can be ours only to the degree we live eyes wide open to all the pain, suffering, and injustice suffusing reality. Moreover, legitimate joy can be ours only to the degree we frankly and without qualification confess our own complicity and culpability in this vale of tears.

In chapter 5, "Concerning Reality: Primordially and Ultimately, 'Yes,'" I explain how faith, and in particular the recognition of a decisive asymmetry in our ethical responsiveness unveils *the reality of a primordial and ultimate "yes" to*

Genesis (i.e., the narratives of the seven days of creation; Adam and Eve; Eve, the serpent, and Adam; the flood; the rainbow covenant; and the tower of Babel).

existence—though we definitely say an impassioned "no" to the enduring pain, suffering, and injustice suffusing existence.[31] In chapter 6, "Concerning Others and Ourselves: Primordially and Ultimately, 'Yes,'" I explain how faith, and in particular grace, delivers forgiveness and thereby *a primordial and ultimate "yes" to others and to ourselves*—though we definitely say an impassioned "no" to others' and our own enduring complicity and culpability.

In part 3, "Fyodor Dostoevsky and Joy Eyes Wide Open to Evil," I strive to facilitate awakening by engaging two celebrated works of literature that address the spiritual challenge of evil in profound and moving narratives. Namely, I strive to unfold the dynamics of faith's saving response to the spiritual challenge of evil in conversation with two acclaimed philosopher/novelists. First, in conversation with Iris Murdoch's valiant but ultimately abortive *The Unicorn*. Second, in conversation with what is arguably the most profound articulation of the spiritual challenge of affirmation in the face of evil in modern Western thought, Fyodor Dostoevsky's brilliant *The Brothers Karamazov*. I am profoundly grateful to Dostoevsky, because *The Brothers Karamazov* (together with the work of Levinas) inspired and informed me as I struggled to understand how agape allows us to meet the spiritual challenge of affirmation in the face of evil.

In chapter 7, "A Cautionary Tale: Iris Murdoch on the Death of the Atomistic 'I,'" I engage the celebrated philosopher and novelist Iris Murdoch. I chose Murdoch because her intentions are so very similar to the intentions of we who strive to defend moral realism in the face of modern Western eliding of moral reality. In particular, Murdoch means to defend moral realism while articulating how "perfect love" delivers a form of immanent salvation. Unfortunately, while Murdoch rightly discerns the modern Western atomistic "I" as a profound obstacle to awakening to love, her "perfect love" falls shy of awakening to the reality of agape, and as a result she is ultimately unable to find her way through to primordial and ultimate affirmation of world, others, and ourselves.

In chapter 8, "Awakening in Dostoevsky: Markel and *The Brothers Karamazov*," I focus on the character of Markel Zosima, the mustard seed at the spiritual heart and narrative turning point of *The Brothers Karamazov*. It is Markel who utters the seemingly hard saying so often repeated by Levinas, "verily each one of us is guilty before everyone, for everyone and everything." This is, amazingly and significantly, the unmitigated confession that delivers unto Markel not condemnation but joy: "Thus he awoke every day with more and more tenderness, rejoicing and all atremble with love," proclaiming, "Am I not in paradise now?"[32]

In brief, Markel is the literary figure of one saved through faith in God, that is, the literary figure of an I who lives surrender to having been seized in and by love, the figure of an I who, living in the light of that love, is saved precisely

---

31. In chapter 8, "A Knowing Idealism: The Decisive Asymmetry," in *For the Love of All Creatures*, I unfold the decisive asymmetry in conversation with the primeval history of Genesis (125–41).

32. Fyodor Dostoevsky, *The Brothers Karamazov: A Novel in Four Parts with Epilogue*, trans. Richard Pevear and Larissa Volokhonsky (New York: Vintage Classics, 1991), 289–90.

insofar as he abandons all thought of self-justification and self-righteousness through radical confession of his own complicity and culpability in this vale of tears. I strive to make clear the difference between those who find salvation through faith that is the gift of grace, as illustrated in Markel, and the straits of those who are caught in devastating, hopeless, self-incurved existential and/ or moral stances, as illustrated by the tragic figures of Murdoch's Effingham Cooper and Dostoevsky's Ivan Karamazov.

In chapter 9, "Joy Eyes Wide Open to Evil: Grace and the Paradise of 'Yes,'" I continue to detail the contrasts among Effingham, Ivan, and Markel, with particular focus on the relationship between confession and salvation. In particular, I attempt to make movingly visible the dynamics of the paradox of wondrous deliverance into the paradise of "yes" that comes with unmitigated confession of complicity and culpability. In the end, I strive to make clear how Markel, facing imminent death, eyes wide open to his own complicity and culpability, eyes wide open to all the evil suffusing reality, is not overwhelmed by "no" but, living in the light of primordial and ultimate affirmation, living surrender to having been seized in and by love for all others, can rejoice eyes wide open in the paradise of "yes."

In chapter 10, "Death's Gift to Life: Living Now Eternally," I consider how and why the proximity of his own death brought the gift of grace to Dostoevsky's Markel, while the proximity of death brought only a brief, shining, but essentially confused and ultimately hapless experience of "perfect love" to Murdoch's Effingham Cooper. Finally, I consider times for mourning and also the possibilities of finding warm comfort even in the face of literal death.

In summary, I explain theoretically (especially in light of the insights of Emmanuel Levinas) and illustrate literarily (especially in light of Dostoevsky's *The Brothers Karamazov*) how faith that is the gift of grace enables joyful, if precisely qualified, affirmation of the world, of others, and of ourselves, and even legitimates moments when we revel in pure joy. More precisely, *in response to the spiritual challenge of affirmation in the face of all the pain, suffering, and injustice suffusing reality, remaining wholly within the bounds of what is generally considered to be reasonable and good (i.e., within the bounds of general revelation), and keeping our eyes wide open to all the enduring evil and also to our own complicity and culpability, I strive to make clear how faith in God, that is, how living surrender to having been seized in and by love, gifts us with a primordial and ultimate "yes" to existence, to others, and to ourselves, and even—without denial, without closing our eyes—legitimates moments when we wholly revel in pure joy.*

PART 1
MODERN WESTERN
EVASIONS OF EVIL

Chapter 1

Unwitting Evasion

Suffering and Righteous Rejection of God

One way modern Westerners evade the challenge posed by the overwhelming reality of evil is—and this may sound counterintuitive at first—by rejecting God in protest. For significant streams of modern Western reflection that emerged in Europe in an overwhelmingly Christian context, the problem of evil was turned into a problem for God instead of a problem for us. In this vein of reflection, it is easy for moral offense over the preponderance of pain, suffering, and injustice in the world to lead to vehement rejection of God. Given the degree of evil suffusing reality, this passionate protest against God is understandable. Ultimately, however, it is an evasion of the spiritual challenge of evil. It acts as a cloak by creating the illusion that the problem of evil is a problem for God and not a problem for us. The spiritual challenge of evil, for atheists as much as for believers, is properly manifest only after this illusion is pierced.

To pierce the illusion one can note the reality and energy of "God" in the passionate protest, which remains in vital play even among those ostensibly rejecting God. That is, God remains definitively in play when one rejects God in bitter protest. This point becomes more apparent once God is truly and wholly removed from the equation. Consistently, remove God, whose existence is purportedly being wholeheartedly rejected, from the passionate protest. Retain all the despair and bitter protest being directed at God but (for the sake of argument) drop God. God does not exist. There is no God.

Now what remains? Notably, there is still all the very same suffering, injustice, and evil, and so also the very same degree of despair and bitter protest. But protest to whom? To whom or what can the protest now be directed? What is to be done with all that passionate energy? *Now all that energy, which was directed against God, must be directed against the cosmos itself, against existence itself, and insofar as we are part and parcel of that existence, against we ourselves.* Therein the devastating spiritual challenge of evil, a challenge to affirmation of existence and ourselves, is manifest. That is the devastating challenge cloaked by passionate and in a sense righteous protest against God.

When the devastating challenge is cloaked, the passionate protest and rejection of God can be treated and experienced as a safe and settled existential stopping point, as if the challenge of evil has dissipated, as if one is no longer afflicted by evil, as if the real spiritual challenge of evil is not just now coming into view. That is, for the protest to work—most especially for the one rejecting God, for the one rejecting the existence of God—God must be real. For the reality of the very God ostensibly being rejected remains integral to the emotional dynamics of the protest against God. "God" plays a real role in the emotional dynamics of the bitter rejection by providing a sort of emotional black hole that absorbs one's despair and anger over the pain, suffering, and injustice, a black hole that can absorb one's emotions (however illusory the process might be), a black hole into which one can unleash all one's despair and anger over the evil and injustice. This is a complex form of denial that can indeed—at a superficial level, so long as the delusion is not pierced—protect us from the implications of the harsh reality of evil, from the spiritual challenge of evil.

Once all this is unmasked, however, once God is wholly and truly rejected, the real spiritual challenge of evil comes into view. Again, reject God and what remains? What remains is precisely the bitter and passionate protest. What are we to do with all that passionate energy? What are we to do with the spiritual dare it hurls at us? To state the angst far too prosaically, how in the face of that protest do we affirm existence, others, and ourselves?

My prose is far too sterile. I am not speaking here of a considered judgment, or of a calculation or evaluation that one self-consciously makes and may decide to change. I am speaking more of a brute moral orientation within this vale of tears. One can work to turn away from all the pain, suffering, and evil. One can resist the feelings, deny the reality. But such efforts themselves betray the truth: the gripping, devastating realization that existence is suffused with pain, suffering, and injustice.

I recall riding in an elevator at the MD Anderson Cancer Center. The doors opened, and a family walked in with a baby who was obviously very ill. A profound sadness, exhaustion, and hopelessness entered the elevator with them. The doors closed and the elevator began its rapid descent. It was clear from their eyes, the silence, the breathing, and something beyond anything I might name that this child was soon to die. There are babies dying every minute.

On another occasion I was attending a birthday party for a friend when I got a call that Clayton, the four-year-old son of another friend, had suddenly died of spinal meningitis, a disease that in his case masked itself as ordinary flu until almost the last moment. A week before little Clayton had been perfectly healthy and playing with us in the gym. These were two different sets of friends. My friends at the birthday party and my friend, the father of Clayton, may have known of each other, but they were not close. When the brief call informing me that Clayton had died ended, I looked up and I was still at the birthday party. I was happy that others were celebrating. I had no desire to dampen their celebration. But I was consumed with grief.

We are afflicted on such occasions. We do not judge something to be awful and then feel terrible. These realities seize us at a level more primordial than considered judgments. We may turn away, resist, deny, but such efforts themselves reveal the reality of our primordial moral sensitivities. All who have lived for a time have their own stories. Many are unbearable to hear. The walls separating us from the child in the oncology unit, the miles separating us from the bedroom where the abused child cries: those walls and miles are not morally relevant. Insofar as we are awake, morally we are all always at the scene of the rape and murder, we are all always beside the nursery bed in the oncology ward, beside the sobbing mothers and fathers at the morgue. Insofar as we are awake, not only to joy but also to overwhelming horror, how do we meet the moral and spiritual challenge, the massive, oppressive, frightful challenge of evil? How can we affirm reality? How do we not direct the bitter, passionate protest onto reality and, insofar as we are part and parcel of this reality, onto others and ourselves?

One common way of dealing with the challenge, of course, is simply to dodge it. We say, "that's life" or "time heals all wounds." Or we steel ourselves against the evil and force our attention elsewhere, looking only at pretty flowers and *Leave It to Beaver* realities. Or we simply dull our moral sensitivities to the point where the spiritual challenge of evil loses force. These may all be somewhat effective coping strategies, but they are also all forms of denial: they all involve denying or suppressing our most profound moral sensitivities.

As I hope is now becoming clear, the passionate and in a sense righteous rejection of the existence of a God whom we nonetheless continue to address in protest is actually a complex and unwitting maneuver by virtue of which we protect ourselves, a maneuver by virtue of which we keep the awful challenge from redounding to us, by virtue of which we divert attention from the spiritual challenge of evil. Wholly apart from and without God, however, the reality of evil clearly presents a challenge to any affirmation of existence, others, and ourselves. Evil afflicts our souls in the face of all the pain, suffering, and injustice. It creates the spiritual challenge that haunts all who are morally awake.

In more ordinary moments, of course, we typically avoid the spiritual challenge of evil by directing our attention away from the more devastating moral realities or by dampening our moral sensitivities. We tend to be fully alive to the reality of evil only when it touches us directly. When we experience moral offense most keenly—often this is not when we are ourselves afflicted but when we are close witnesses—we may deal with the challenge of evil by masking it. Attacks on a God in whom we do not believe may be the most common and potent form of such masking. Such attacks are especially common and psychologically understandable in extreme circumstances. Indeed, such a reaction is explicitly acknowledged in lamentations found in the Hebrew Scriptures, though in the Scriptures, most reasonably and very significantly, the despairing lamentations and accusations are hurled against a God in whom you still believe, even against a God in whom, in some still distant day, you might yet again hope.

Given the power of our moral sensitivities and the harsh realities of this world, our primordial desire to mask the apparently unanswerable, devastating challenge of affirmation in this vale of tears is entirely understandable. Recall, among many such examples, the horrible tsunami that struck the rim of the Indian Ocean on December 26, 2004. In the subsequent days and months I read only a couple accounts of what happened: the three-year-old boy sucked from his father's arms and out to sea, never to be seen again; the mother who realized in one instant that she could not hold onto both of her little children before the power of the retreating wave, who realized that to attempt to save both would be to lose both, who in that horrifying, unthinkable instant chose which of her two beloved children she would cling to with both arms and save, and which she would release to the sea.

The accounts were overwhelming. And those were two stories involving five people, all total strangers to me. *Two hundred and thirty thousand* people were killed, along with multitudes of other creatures. Each carried his or her own story. Who could possibly bear intimate acquaintance with all of those stories, all of those victims, all of that horror, suffering, and loss?

Of course, I also delighted and found solace in the stories of heroism and survival, in tales of remarkable rescues and unexpectedly reunited families. I read happily the oft-told story of the people of one village, themselves survivors of the tsunami, who saved a stranded and orphaned baby hippo, a hippo who proceeded to adopt, and to be adopted by, an old tortoise as its friend and surrogate mother.[1]

While I found some solace in the stories of rescue and goodness, however, I would never even begin to try to *calculate* the good versus the bad, to suggest to that father or mother that on the whole it was worth it. This is a realm in which the application of any calculus of utility becomes obscene. There is no measure that is appropriate, no measuring that is appropriate. To adopt the existential stance necessary to look and measure, even if one had an infinitely subtle calculus,

---

1. I am referring to the famous baby hippo, Owen, who was adopted by a century-old tortoise, Mzee, after the tsunami. Innumerable accounts of the tale are available online.

would be an offense, for it would be the willing of oneself to a psychopathic, willed nonresponsiveness, a willed rejection of our response-ability.

In the face of such horrors to pause, to break existentially from one's moral sensitivities, forcefully to put them in check and to contain them as objects to be controlled and used when and as one wills, would itself be a moral offense. That is why Dostoevsky, when seeking to awaken this depth of moral sensitivity in *The Brothers Karamozov*, tells us the heart-breaking tale of one small girl—alone, shattered, beaten, and betrayed by her very own parents—and then suggests that, taken by the tears of that one child, we cannot but reject the world as hopelessly offensive.[2] The heart truly possessed by so refined a moral sensitivity, so complete a love for others, is not so hardened that it only breaks when rejoined with tales of the Holocaust or of an epochal tsunami. Nor does it pause to make any calculations—such would be obscene. One is moved utterly and beyond any calculation by the hurt and tears of that single child.

Let me confess that this infinitely high and sustained moral sensitivity is not one to which I lay personal claim. I have a sense for the attractiveness of the denial involved in protecting oneself from the devastating "*No!*" that flows from our most profound moral sensitivities. In response to the Indian Ocean tsunami on that day after Christmas 2004, I for the most part did something agreeably soft. The 230,000 were too many. Unfathomable. Overwhelming. So I dampened my moral sensibilities. I did not want the pain to continue or increase. I really wanted it to soften and disappear. So I did not seek out more news about the devastation. I certainly did not forget the event, but I did what I could to keep it to the margins of my consciousness. I attended to other things. Within a week I managed to be fairly, though far from wholly, forgetful and happy as I celebrated New Year's Eve.

Is that not worse—less morally sensitive, less morally honest—than the case of those who spent the week cursing God? Even if they were protecting themselves by using "God" to shield from themselves the full depths of the horror, were they nonetheless not more honest and alive to the moral reality and to the spiritual challenge of affirmation?

Very few, probably none, can sustain anguished cursing of God or cosmos, let alone of self. For perfectly understandable reasons many of us sooner or later dampen our moral sensitivities just so we can live out and to some degree enjoy our daily lives. We sit somberly through the funeral on Friday afternoon, and then we have some fun at the birthday party Saturday evening. We all know, or know that we really do not want to know, the statistics on child abuse, rape, spousal abuse, cancer deaths, highway deaths, global poverty, starvation, malaria, sex trafficking, and the ongoing slaughter in wars. We all know, or know that we really do not want to know, about the factory farms and the animal experimentation, about wild fish and birds sick and dying because

---

2. In the novel, Ivan Karamazov tells the story. For reasons I will detail in chapter 8, Ivan's morality is devastatingly truncated.

of toxic waters. We all know that at any given moment there are unbearable tragedies playing themselves out on our highways, in living rooms and bedrooms around our neighborhood, in local emergency rooms and hospital wards, in research centers, and in spider webs and birds' nests in back yards. Temporal and spatial distances are not morally significant, and so they offer no legitimate protection (though they may facilitate denial). Spiritually, all of the suffering is immediately before and with us.

SURVIVOR GUILT

Taken alone, full moral awareness of all the evil, suffering, and injustice suffusing reality should put us into a spiritual state that may best be imagined in terms of "survivor guilt."[3] Survivor guilt is the feeling of survivors of the Holocaust, the tsunami, the plane crash, or the automobile accident. These survivors do not merely logically acknowledge, but at the core of their being they realize that others have suffered or died while they remain alive, not by virtue of any special right or distinguishing trait but by sheer chance. Overwhelmed by their fortuitous survival when all surrounding them have suffered and died, survivors can suddenly find any assertion of their right to exist, any assertion of a right to their "place in the sun" (Pascal) utterly unthinkable, even repulsive.[4]

These survivors are caught. For their sheer existence, their very continuing-to-breathe, constitutes an unwilled assertion of a right to exist. Their ongoing existence, their mere living, now afflicts them with a burden, for it is an inescapable, de facto, pre-intentional, unasserted assertion of being that is carried in their ongoing existence. Their ongoing existence stands as an assertion that they now have no desire or inclination to make as an assertion, a claim that they now no longer feel they have any right to make, but an assertion still made by them insofar as they in fact continue to live, insofar as they continue to occupy their "place in the sun." The de facto, pre-intentional assertion of be-ing involved in their very existing is now sensed as unwarranted: survivor guilt.

Survivor guilt is not guilt over actions but guilt over be-ing, over living itself. It is guilt whose source is deeper than any mere bad act that one may intentionally commit. Before and apart from any intention, one finds oneself complicit, guilty, responsible. This is a responsibility more primordial than the

---

3. The idea for using "survivor guilt" comes from Emmanuel Levinas, who typically spoke of this reality in terms of "bad conscience" but who in one interview talked of "the guilty survivor" in an attempt to be more easily understood (Levinas, "The Philosopher and Death," in Emmanuel Levinas, *Is It Righteous to Be? Interviews with Emmanuel Levinas*, ed. Jill Robbins [Stanford: Stanford University Press, 2001], 126).

4. Blaise Pascal, *Pensées*, as cited in Emmanuel Levinas, *Otherwise Than Being, or Beyond Essence*, trans. Alphonso Lingis (Pittsburgh: Duquesne University Press, 1981), vii. The "thoughts" are numbered differently in various collections of Pascal's works. What Levinas numbers as thought number 112 is thought number 295 in the Brunschvicg edition and is thought number 64 (page 47) of the Penguin edition translated by A. J. Krailsheimer (New York, 1966).

responsibility one feels for acts that one has freely chosen, but for that reason this is a more primordial, more devastating responsibility.[5]

Survivor guilt typically results from some extreme event in which the utterly and radically serendipitous character of your survival is brutally and immediately juxtaposed with the violent death of innocents. In this sort of survivor guilt, a reality blunted in typical day-to-day existence by temporal and spatial distance is made radically present and immediate. *In reality, rejecting the morally illegitimate blunting of sensitivities that results from temporal or spatial distance, we should all experience survivor guilt. For in fully inhabited moral reality, in our spiritual standing alongside all others, the safe distances created by time and space are not relevant.* In the eternal, supra-spatial-temporal, living *now* of moral be-ing, the nightmares suffered at this moment even on the other side of an ocean are right here with me. In the eternal, supra-spatial-temporal, living *now* of moral be-ing, the horrors of Auschwitz, now more than half a century distant, are right now with me.

We typically accede before thinking to the illicit, moral blunting-effect of space and time, a blunting that hides the truth, that cloaks the overwhelming reality, that facilitates a naive and blissfully ignorant persevering in our be-ing, that preserves us in lives wherein happiness is purchased—at least for a time—at the price of moral superficiality. Such superficiality may be pierced when our lives or our sensitivities become more intense, or perhaps we might manage to persevere in self-enclosed, superficial bliss until, in an unanticipated instant, all perseverance and thought simply stop (i.e., when sudden death takes us by surprise).

I am not denying the existence of a real psychopathology labeled "survivor guilt," which should be addressed by a professional psychologist or psychiatrist. That psychological survivor guilt is different from spiritual survivor guilt. The survivor guilt under consideration here is not the product of pathology or of confusion. It is the result of utter, clear, unblinking openness to searing moral truth. It is a truth that penetrates our consciousness most powerfully and clearly amid extreme circumstances. But while such circumstances heighten our sensitivities and penetrate veils of denial or neglect, it is our consciousness that is variable, not the truth. What is apparently the searing and global moral truth is a constant: it is not righteous for us to be.

Even with regard to nonpathological, spiritual survivor guilt, it is not unusual to hear well-meaning friends counsel that one needs space and time in order to get distance from the pivotal event; others may strive to return you to a place where you can once again assert confidently your right to be. You may even seek to regain a distance sufficient to retrieve a measure of superficial bliss. When one lives in the eternal, supra-spatial-temporal, living *now* of spiritual be-ing, however, when Darfur, Auschwitz, the tsunami, the earthquakes, the tears of a child unloved and beaten, the whimpering of the physically beaten and

---

5. This would be what Levinas refers to as a "more ancient" responsibility or guilt.

emotionally wounded dog, or the quaking of the tortured, eyelid-less bunny, when all these live right now, right here with you, then you realize that survivor guilt—far from a rare and unfortunate condition to be avoided if possible and treated if necessary—offers a window into a raw truth of reality. Again, the sort of survivor guilt I am describing here does not name a psychological malady, illness, confusion, or delusion. It names awakening to moral truth. To be morally awake is not to be ill, it is to be honest, utterly clear, and unblinkingly alive to moral reality and the horrors suffusing existence.

Until one moves, defenses down, eyes open wide to the death, suffering, and despair that suffuse reality as surely and constantly as the love, beauty, and joy—that is, until one moves *into* survivor guilt, which stands not as a reality to be avoided but as a truth to be realized, a moment to be inhabited fully, one is treading a path of delusion. For any other be-ing is predicated on denial of the truth, willful aversion to reality. Any other be-ing is predicated on a lie, a delusion of innocence, a lie one must constantly reassert and reinforce, a lie one must tell to oneself, to others, most likely with others, *continually*. For we are indeed spiritual, we are indeed response-able, and so we are continually reminded by life, by our encounter with all sorts of creatures calling out to us, we are continually reminded of the moral truth. In our daily lives a host of creatures continually call out to us, continually prod us toward awakening. So the denial must be reasserted and reinforced continually.

The denial is completely understandable, for it seems impossible to live continually and fully attuned to the reality of evil. It seems impossible to be morally honest and yet to escape the judgment that it is not righteous to be. To be fully and continually vulnerable to the horror, pain, and suffering feels just unbearable. But there is no morally honest opting out of the harsh realities in this vale of tears. Our denial, our masking, the relief of inattention—all these are understandable reactions, but they are also dishonest, self-deceptive, unreal. Are we caught forever between the options of either dishonest living or searing honesty? Is there no escape? Is there no possibility of honest affirmation?

The temptation, one to which modernity (largely unwittingly) succumbed with a vengeance, is to succumb to the fear that there is no way out, and so to mask the brutal spiritual challenge. Following the spiritual wisdom of Fyodor Dostoevsky and Emmanuel Levinas, I will be striving to unfold the possibility of joyful life without denial, without escape, and without inattention. I will be striving to unfold the possibility of life lived fully alive to our most primordial moral sensitivities, life lived facing square-on not only wonders but also horrors.

Let me avoid raising any false hopes by reiterating that I will offer no magical escape from our recognition of and horror over the evil suffusing reality, no magic pill that suddenly makes everything okay or provides us with a pretty, ribbon-wrapped picture of reality. Nonetheless, I will in the end indeed testify to a miracle: to celebration of life without denial, to celebration of life that remains supremely sensitive to all the moral horrors and suffering and injustice, but simultaneously, to life full of affirmation and joy. Some may judge the hope I proffer too thin. In any case, I resolve to proceed with utter honesty, for the first and overriding commitment of this exploration is to frank and honest awakening to and acknowledgment of our most profound and sure moral sensitivities, a commitment to be frank and honest before both the wonders and the horrors that bless and afflict creatures and creation, a commitment to keep our eyes wide open to the pain, suffering, and injustice suffusing this vale of tears—no evasion, no denial. This commitment comes before a commitment to a happy ending. For there is no honest opting out of our moral sensitivities, no legitimate evasion of survivor guilt. Insofar as there is a legitimate path to affirmation, it must *pass through acceptance of responsibility and acknowledgment that we have no right to be.* Morally honest joy must be joy had while our eyes remain wide open to evil.

In this chapter I have identified and unraveled one common form of evasion, evasion gained through passionate rejection of God on moral grounds. The challenge of evil to affirmation is so powerful and threatening, however, that myriad forms of evasion have developed in modern Western culture. So before exploring the possibility of moving *through* survivor guilt to joy, in the next three chapters I will explore three additional modern Western conceptual trajectories that confusedly shield us from the spiritual challenge of evil. In chapters 3 and 4 ("Biocentrism and Faces: Deep Ecology and The Land Ethic" and "Aldo Leopold and the Wolf: A Confession Betrayed") I will respond to the holistic, nature-loving spirituality of Arne Naess's "deep ecology" and of Aldo Leopold's "land ethic." First, however, I will return to the immensely influential nineteenth century philosopher who mistakenly concluded that "opting out" of our moral sensitivities was the only path to affirmation in the face of all the evil suffusing this world, a philosopher who remained, despite himself, morally vulnerable and tortured: Friedrich Nietzsche.

Chapter 2

Salvation after
the Death of God
Nietzsche

AFFIRMATION WITHOUT GOD

"The wisest men in every age have reached the same conclusion about life: *it's no good*."[1] So concludes Friedrich Nietzsche in *Twilight of the Idols*. Nietzsche concludes that in order to escape this judgment concerning life, "*it's no good*," most philosophies and religions have appealed to one fantastic otherworldly realm or another. On Nietzsche's reading, the philosopher Arthur Schopenhauer, who, like Nietzsche himself, rejected all religious appeals, was admirable because he faced the challenge without flinching and without abandoning reality. But Schopenhauer did not overcome the challenge, and as a result his philosophy was profoundly pessimistic. Nietzsche judges Schopenhauer's pessimism to be more honest but no more acceptable than what he sees as the flights to fantasy called "religion," for Nietzsche craves and demands affirmation of life. So Nietzsche takes a radical step: he proposes we meet the severity of the spiritual challenge with an equally severe transvaluation of the West's most treasured values. This

---

1. Friedrich Nietzsche, *The Anti-Christ, Ecce Homo, Twilight of the Idols, and Other Writings*, trans. A. Judith Norman, ed. Aaron Ridley (Cambridge: Cambridge University Press, 2005), 162.

transvaluation is not a change in values but the wholesale extirpation of any moral sensitivity—a move totally beyond good and evil.

In short, Nietzsche suggests we opt out of acknowledging the reality of evil. Tellingly, when he discusses the need to transvalue our moral valuing, he speaks of the need to "self-overcome" our moral sensitivities in order to be able to say "yes" to all that is (just as it is). This is telling because it means that Nietzsche does not deny our moral sensitivities. To the contrary, he describes the overcoming of them, their erasure, as a herculean task, a work of generations that will take centuries.

Nietzsche thinks our classic moral sensitivities are wholly sociocultural products, indeed, that they are largely unconscious instruments of control limiting those who are strongest and most excellent, and thus that they are infinitely malleable and that their elimination is both possible and desirable. In the wake of the challenge to provide some justification of the cosmos, one can understand why this Nietzschean proposal would be attractive to those who are relatively powerful in society and eager to shed and/or discredit the qualms and claims generated by their own moral sensitivities.

It is not surprising, then, that among many modern Western cultural elites there has been overt affirmation of the hegemony of the aesthetic (the ubiquity of taste) over and against the moral. The moral has come to be seen as wholly derivative, wholly epiphenomenal, a species of the aesthetic. In short, a powerful trajectory among mainstream Western intellectual elites has accepted Nietzsche's contention that moral realism is a fiction, and they have tried to make his recommended transvaluation of values a sociocultural reality by eliding moral realism as a conceptual category and insisting on viewing all values as aspects of the aesthetic and/or as wholly sociocultural products.

Clearly, our ethical and sociopolitical norms are partly the product of sociocultural conditioning. I will argue, however, that our sociopolitical norms are themselves also partly the product of having been seized in and by love. Thus our having been seized in and by love ultimately if imperfectly reflects an intrinsic dimension of reality, the moral part of reality, the reality of agape. This reality is not ultimately and wholly derivative of the calculus of survival potentials (i.e., wholly Darwinian). It is not merely a function of human language and culture but has helped to shape human language and culture. It is a reality that we do not judge but over and against which we are judged. If this is correct, and if our moral sensitivities and sociopolitical norms are themselves also partly the product of a moral reality, then Nietzsche's transvaluation is not merely incredibly difficult for any individual to achieve. It is impossible in principle. For then Nietzsche's transvaluation is a denial of that which exists before and beyond any of our efforts, a denial of a reality that, far from ultimately reflecting the contours of socio-cultural conditioning, ultimately and continually conditions each one of us and our cultures. If that is the case, then the *Übermenschen*, Nietzsche's "super humans," who have supposedly "self-overcome" classic convictions about good and evil, that is, who have successfully closed themselves off to having been seized in and by love for the Faces of others, are not enlightened but deranged—they willfully strive after psychopathology.

Nietzsche deliberately offers a morally unacceptable alternative because, of course, the whole point is to defeat the spiritually devastating threat of our moral sensitivities. In a sense, the goal of this son and grandson of Lutheran ministers is pastoral. The transvaluation of morals is meant to be an alternative means to the ends of grace, a means that proceeds by jettisoning the source of the guilt that makes grace necessary. Transvaluing values is meant to be an alternative, empowering way to step beyond guilt and to achieve full self-affirmation, a way to say "yes" to self and to reality after the death of God. Of course, in marked contrast to classic Jewish and Christian spirituality (and, for that matter, the spirituality of the Islamic, Hindu, Buddhist, and many other traditions), for Nietzsche this "grace" is now *intended* rather than humbly accepted; it comes through assertion, not confession. Nietzschean "grace" is achieved when you wholly "self-overcome," (i.e., obliterate) your primordial moral sensitivities so that you can say "yes" to all that is.

Since Nietzsche means to reject classic morality, pointing out the amorality or immorality of his position is not a convincing counterargument. It simply restates an aspect of his position and persuades only to the degree that it surreptitiously begs the critical question. However, without begging any questions, one can counter Nietzsche by noting he most certainly has failed to prove that our moral sensitivities are wholly malleable, sociocultural products that can be obliterated.

One can also, in good Nietzschean fashion, worry that there may be a potent and illicit ideological component afflicting him and others who defend his position, since it protects them from the threat of moral condemnation. After all, what can easily accompany the self-overcoming of our primordial moral sensitivities is a very attractive personal assurance of our own innocence, a shield from any moral accusation—an attractive option for many (especially those who are benefitting from the oppression of others). That is, the Nietzschean, amoral surrogate for grace may be attractive for illicit, self-centered, unethical reasons.

In sum, Nietzsche offers an alternative that is neither warranted by the discoveries of modern science nor demanded by unprejudiced reason. Moreover, he offers an alternative that runs counter to humanity's most profound moral sensitivities and offers its adherents profound existential protection from moral condemnation via denial of moral reality. *There is, then, not only no strong reason to accede to a Nietzschean transvaluation of values, but there are also profound ethical reasons to be suspicious of any inclination one might feel toward it.*

While it has little argumentative weight, it is perhaps to Nietzsche's unwitting credit that he himself was famously unable to suppress his own most profound moral sensitivities. I suspect one powerful reason Nietzsche felt the burden of moral sensitivities that could not be fulfilled was that he himself —a one-time divinity student, son and grandson of Lutheran ministers—had keenly developed moral sensitivities that, in the wake of his loss of faith, he experienced as crushing.

There is a famous story that traditionally marks the moment when Nietzsche succumbed to full-blown insanity (the product of an undiagnosed disease of the brain). In 1888, Nietzsche, who was known generally for his sensitivity to nonhuman animals, saw an abused horse struggling to pull some sort of public conveyance in Turin, Italy. Breaking down in tears, Nietzsche raced over and embraced the poor creature, most likely in order to shield her from the whip.[2] One cannot make too much of such a story, but taken together with his general concern for nonhuman animals, and also taken together with the profound moral sensitivities that Nietzsche, despite himself, betrayed in the energy of his antimoral tirades and in his call for "self-overcoming," there is reason to suspect that even Nietzsche, had he not fallen ill, may eventually have come to reject his own amoral recommendations.

Indeed, this gives us some reason to suspect that Nietzsche was not only never quite an accomplished Nietzschean, but even that he was never quite convinced of Nietzscheanism. This gives us some reason to suspect that there may be a place for a subtle and sympathetic reading of his work against its explicit grain, reason to suspect that if illness had not taken his mind at the young age of forty-three, if he had reflected and matured and written for another twenty or thirty years, twentieth-century philosophers may well have ended up talking about a dramatic "turn" that distinguished the early from the later Nietzsche.[3]

In any case, we now see how Nietzsche represents one influential response to the spiritual challenge of evil. Instead of answering the monumental challenge, Nietzsche recommends we dissolve it by eliminating our primordial moral sensitivities. This is his alternative means of grace, his path to salvation after the death of God. Let me try to make all this more concrete with an illustration.

LION, GAZELLE, FACES

The scenario is familiar, and most of us can bring the scene to mind. The video begins with a beautiful, placid scene. A herd of doe-brown gazelles, youngsters leaping and dashing playfully to and fro, graze on a grassy plain. The music changes as the camera zooms in on the tall grass in the background. First the ears and then the eyes and face of a lion are brought into focus. The lion charges and with impossible quickness the herd is in flight. One gazelle is slower than the rest, and soon he is isolated from the vanishing herd. The lion focuses in. The doe-brown gazelle dashes to and fro desperately yet gracefully. Sudden changes of direction thwart but do not lose the faster but less agile lion. The gazelle tires and his turns slow. The lion leaps, her front claws tear into and catch in the

2. Lesley Chamberlain, *Nietzsche in Turin: An Intimate Biography* (New York: Picador USA, 1999), 207–8.

3. For a good account of this period see chapter 11, "Collapse Into the Beyond," of Chamberlain's *Nietzsche in Turin*. A Christian can (and, I would argue, *should*) affirm Nietzsche's diagnosis and critique of *ressentiment* without identifying it with the best trajectories of Christian understanding.

gazelle's back, gazelle and lion tumble and roll into a haze of dust. Out of the haze the lion emerges, the limp gazelle gripped in her jaws.

In accord with having been seized in and by love for every Face, we see at best here a necessary tragedy (i.e., "necessary" given the biological demands for survival in this world). In this scenario, we feel first for the desperation, pain, terror, and loss of the gazelle. In another documentary, however, we may have been invited to the perspective of the lion. Perhaps she has cubs, has been unsuccessful in her hunts, and this represents her last, desperate attempt to find the food she and her cubs need if they are to survive. That is, from another perspective we can take joy in the lion's success in the hunt: now that lion will have food for herself and perhaps for her cubs as well. We also bear in mind that lions are carnivores (they must kill and eat in order to survive), and we know that lions typically do kill not for pleasure but only when they must eat in order to survive. In short, this is a necessary tragedy. We mourn the death of the gazelle. We are glad for the lion, but our happiness for the lion is dampened by the tragic (i.e., inescapable but awful) death of the gazelle.

Nietzsche would see our moral sensitivities here, our having been seized in and by love for the lion and for the gazelle, and most especially our mourning for the gazelle, as devastating weakness. For in a world overwhelmingly and irremediably suffused with tragedy, those too weak to self-overcome their moral sensitivities will be forced to conclude with "the wisest men in every age" concerning life: "it's no good."[4] To be perfectly clear and fair, I should stress that the problem is *not*, for Nietzsche, that this weakness will inhibit us from exploiting others when we have the chance. Nietzsche may well leave us with weakened resources for condemning such exploitation, and many have appropriated Nietzsche to add philosophical legitimacy to their exploitation, but Nietzsche clearly was not meaning to sanction blatant injustice or oppression. Nietzsche was not a proto-Nazi. The *Übermensch* may *choose* to take pity on those beneath him or her. Nietzsche clearly preferred that people so choose. He saw that as the more cultured, the more excellent, the stronger choice for *Übermenschen* to make.[5]

Nietzsche's real concern, however, is to stress that it is a *choice*, a choice made from strength in excellence. His concern is to stress that one should choose and not succumb to any feeling of obligation, not succumb to any sense of call, to any moral sensitivity. We should steel ourselves against any sorrow when we see the lion take the gazelle. In fact, we should so thoroughly obliterate our moral sensitivities that there would be no need to steel ourselves, we would simply and easily turn from the scene, perhaps even talk in sophisticated tones about the awesome beauty of the scene, including the beauty of the suffering and death.

---

4. Nietzsche, *Twilight of the Idols*, 162.

5. To be clear, insofar as I am to some degree admittedly crediting this to Nietzsche as to some degree *good*, I am involving Nietzsche in latent moralizing (and, as I will be suggesting, it seems to me that Nietzsche personally never quite succeeded in achieving the transvaluation of values he recommends).

Consistency dictates that Nietzsche's transvaluation of values be applied not just to that gazelle but also to the beauty of the tsunami, and most specifically to the terrible beauty of the sea's taking of those little children right from their mother's arms. One can actually hear such horrible talk as this on occasion in seemingly polite, pseudo-sophisticated modern conversation, talk of the strength of dispassionately facing up to the destructive character of reality, even talk of the beauty of horror, talk wherein one hears actualized in privileged and sanitized settings the Nietzschean transvaluation, the aesthetic obliteration of the moral.

Nietzsche's antireligious but pastor's worry was that our primordial moral sensitivities preclude full affirmation of ourselves and our world. For the sake of full self-affirmation and maximal joy and achievement, he argued, we must overcome our moral sensitivities, for they turn in our hands and before them we find ourselves irredeemably condemning our world and our selves. For Nietzsche the story of the lion and the gazelle, or even of the mother and her children in the tsunami, could function as a self-diagnostic test. To the degree you feel any moral call you are failing the test, and you need to do more work at transvaluation. The imperative is to feel no compulsion to see tragedy. The key is fully and absolutely to extirpate your moral sensitivities.

Perhaps to his personal credit, let us remember Nietzsche's tears for that poor beaten horse. Nietzsche's own evident inability fully to transvalue his own values provides no conclusive argument against his position. However, it is not insignificant that it takes hard and continual work to deny our most profound moral sensitivities. It is logically possible that we are profoundly and perpetually confused about moral reality. But while the fact that that possibility is virtually impossible to believe is not a conclusive argument against its truth, it surely shifts the burden of proof to those who would affirm such a literally unbelievable possibility.

In fact, there is as of yet simply no substantial reason to conclude that moral reality is wholly a function of biological and sociocultural conditioning (i.e., nature and nurture; genes and memes). The burden of proof still falls squarely on those who would deny the revelatory character of our most profound moral sensitivities, the immediate and powerful reality of having been seized in and by love for Faces. When one adds that burden of proof to ideological concerns over the Nietzschean position (i.e., that it plays to the self-interest of elites by lifting all burden of responsibility for others), one has a strong, non-question-begging argument not only for holding the Nietzschean recommendation in abeyance but also for judging it ethically dangerous, philosophically weak, ideologically encumbered, and morally confused.

There is a complexity here with regard to free will that needs to be clarified. I affirm free will but I oppose the unqualified, modern emphasis on authenticity in terms of radical autonomy, wherein true human authenticity is had only when you refuse to recognize any moral call or any other external force as authoritative and instead strive to live only in accord with your own considered judgment of what is good/preferrable. The problem with this modern demand for radical, unmitigated autonomy is that in fact you do not choose your moral sensitivities; you find yourself seized by them, and your autonomy comes into play vis-à-vis moral reality only in your ability to resist or deny or, on the contrary, to open yourself ever more fully to that reality and to act, or not, in light of its call.

I affirm free will in the ordinary sense, then, but not within a morally neutral context or within a context wherein the only good is self-creation *ex nihilo* (e.g., Sartrean authenticity). This affirmation of autonomy is *real* insofar as it holds that we can affirm or deny, cultivate or resist, act in accord with or contrary to having been seized in and by love, but this affirmation of free will is not *radical* insofar as it holds that the call and reality of having been seized in and by love for Faces reveals a moral reality, the reality of agape, a reality that first seizes us.

SARTRE'S NEO-NIETZSCHEAN ALTERNATIVE

I am criticizing two distinct positions that are intermingled somewhat haphazardly in Nietzsche's thought. First, there is the modern scientific reduction that sees all morality and everything that we confusedly refer to under the heading of "free will" as ultimately a function of blind evolutionary forces, a product of nature or nurture or some combination of the two, perhaps seasoned with sheer randomness. Second, along an incommensurable conceptual trajectory, one that is more famously Nietzschean and developed by Jean-Paul Sartre, I am criticizing radical (but not real) autonomy, the affirmation of individual will within a wholly amoral reality, an affirmation of a will that is authentic only to the degree that it freely chooses not only what to do but also chooses the very standards by which it will judge itself. This is Sartre's atomistic (i.e., each self is radically distinct for Sartre) appropriation of Christianity's "creation out of nothing" (creation *ex nihilo*), the formerly divine prerogative that becomes the prerogative of and a necessity for any self that would be authentic.

In other words, for Sartre any self that would be a self and not a mere vanishing confluence of forces within existence, not only a collection of genes and memes, not a puppet, must define and choose itself *ex nihilo*, must never acknowledge the authority and reality of external norms. Significantly, this Sartrean ideal is famously opposed to the reductionism implicit in the hegemony of modern scientific rationality, which of necessity sees every supposed act of free will in the Sartrean sense of authentic choice as unintelligible hocus-pocus, as no more consonant with modern science and reason than are astrology and belief in miracles. That is, two vaunted affirmations of modern Western thought, namely, affirmation of the unmitigated reach of modern science (which rejects free will) and affirmation of individual autonomy and the ideal of personal authenticity (which requires free will) are conceptually incommensurable.

I think we should affirm Sartre in his affirmation of autonomy and celebration of personal authenticity, but I contend his insistence on moral neutrality—his neo-Nietzschean idea that we can and should, if we are to exist authentically, freely choose what to see as good or evil, rather than freely choosing how to respond to our primordial having been seized—I contend that Sartre's moral neutrality does not accurately reflect the primordial, pre-intentional, prereflective character of our moral sensitivities, wherein we first of all find ourselves seized in and by love for all creatures. I affirm real autonomy, but not Sartre's radical autonomy, for I affirm both free will and moral realism (i.e., an always prior having been seized by moral reality).

CONTRA NIETZSCHE AND SARTRE

For those of us who quite reasonably refuse to disown our primordial moral having been seized, there is nothing morally admirable or reasonable about the Nietzschean spirit when it calls on us to look upon the lion and the gazelle and obliterate any and all sense of sadness, sympathy, or tragedy. Neither is there anything more redeemable in Sartre's neo-Nietzschean trajectory, in accord with which we should, if we are to live authentically, look upon the lion and the gazelle and *choose* our moral responses—again, that is simply not an accurate description of how we are seized morally. Not only are neither Nietzsche nor Sartre's positions morally admirable; neither accurately describes our primordial moral having been seized. As Nietzsche's failure at self-overcoming tellingly illustrates, it is not clear that adapting their recommendations wholesale is even possible (unless one is psychopathic—this is another way of saying that neither appears to be an accurate reflection of reality). The Nietzschean (and Sartrean) options, then, are most reasonably rejected.

In sum, once we are fully alive to primordial having been seized in and by love for all creatures and also to the evil of the violation of any creature, we realize that all the pain, suffering, and injustice suffusing reality confronts us with something even worse than a mortal threat—at a primordial level, to put it in prosaic terms, it threatens our ability to affirm reality, others, and ourselves as good. It threatens us not with death, but with primordial and ultimate condemnation, with a form of survivor guilt. Again, precisely the admirable outrage, which is so often and understandably turned in bitter protest against God, who is then often rejected because of all the evil and suffering, precisely that outrage, *after* the death of God, must now be turned against existence itself, including others and ourselves.

This is precisely the threat Nietzsche perceived with depth and passion, precisely the threat that led him to recommend the radical and for him evidently impossible annihilation of his moral sensitivities. If God is dead, then you cannot reject Nietzsche's immoral amorality without immediately bringing down on yourself a monumental moral challenge, for our most profound moral sensitivities render an unbearable judgment on us. For all the passion and bitterness and invective commonly hurled at God *redounds on us.*

To review, a superficial response to the spiritual challenge of evil is denial, a dampening of our moral sensibilities, a focusing of our attention on what is good and pleasant. Doubtless this is a most common response among those of us privileged or lucky enough to be temporally or spatially distant from the immediate presence of evil and horror. But while such denial is an understandable response—one that will probably always be with us—it is not defensible because it trades on superficiality.

A second, more admirable response is to engage in unwitting diversion by channeling our rage against evil into a rejection of God. But once God is truly rejected the futility of this response is manifest, for we are still left with all the passionate invective, which now turns on the cosmos itself, including us.

A third response to the challenge, the Nietzschean response, urges us to annihilate our moral sensitivities altogether. The Nietzschean response, even if it is incorrect, is profound and warrants consideration because it does not traffic in superficiality. But it can consider itself to be truly tested only in the immediate presence of horrific evil. However, in such contexts—at Auschwitz, in the oncology ward, in the morgue, in the wake of the tsunami—we rightly consider anyone who is not seized morally to be horribly lacking in a most basic and supremely significant human capacity (i.e., to be a psychopath). Furthermore, the Nietzschean response plays to the self-interest of those who are oppressive (though this was not Nietzsche's intent). So one reasonably rejects the Nietzschean recommendation, because it deals with the momentous moral challenge by recommending that we "transvalue" (i.e., annihilate) our moral sensitivities, and also because it lends absolution to and relativizes condemnation of those who benefit from and maintain oppressive (i.e., unjust, Face violating) relations among creatures.

Chapter 3

Biocentrism and Faces

Deep Ecology and the Land Ethic

THE HOLISTIC ALTRUISM OF BIOCENTRISM

I have unfolded two influential modern Western responses to the primordial moral challenge of affirmation. The first was a common evasion based, paradoxically and confusedly, on moral rejection of God. The second was Nietzsche's purportedly salvific, aesthetic eliding of the moral. We now turn to a response that is spiritually profound but ultimately problematic, biocentrism. "Biocentrism" refers to a holistic, non-self-centered, non-selves-centered spirituality central to deep ecology and also to advocates of the land ethic (and to some who advocate for the Gaia hypothesis). My concern in this section is not deep ecology or the land ethic per se, but biocentric spirituality—a spirituality whose character will be familiar to anyone who has ever found themselves overwhelmed, self-forgetful, and awed by vast vistas of sky, mountains, desert, or ocean.

Norwegian philosopher and mountaineer Arne Naess coined the phrase "deep ecology."[1] Naess was deeply influenced by the naturalistic seventeenth

1. Other major figures in the deep ecology movement include Gary Snyder, Bill Devall, and George Sessions, who appeal to the thought of Henry David Thoreau, John Muir, and D. H.

century Dutch philosopher Baruch Spinoza. Though it has a distinct conceptual pedigree, deep ecology is very close in its biocentric spirit to early twentieth century American conservationist Aldo Leopold's celebrated "land ethic." In his landmark work, *A Sand County Almanac*, Leopold famously concludes that, "a thing is right when it tends to preserve the integrity, stability, and beauty of the biotic community. It is wrong when it tends otherwise."[2]

Biocentrism offers a different way of transvaluing our classic moral sensitivities and saying "yes" to all that is. In stark contrast to Nietzsche, who sees our classic moral sensitivities as enervating, poisoning our affirmation of and concern for ourselves, biocentrism finds our classic moral intuitions to be too selves-centered. For instance, where Nietzsche seeks to overcome the altruism celebrated by and energizing our classic moral sensitivities, biocentrism radicalizes altruism beyond even the classic Western religious ideal (e.g., of Platonism, Judaism, Christianity, or Islam), which focuses concern on all *individuals* (including one's self).

Perhaps it is not coincidental that Arne Naess was a serious mountaineer, for deep ecology reflects the spirituality typically engendered by prolonged and intense sojourns in mountain extremes. Given sufficient time and isolation high up in the mountains, it is easy to lose track of oneself, easy even to lose track of concern for oneself. One becomes so focused on and attuned to the surpassing beauty, majesty, and rhythm of the rivers, canyons, peaks, forest, clouds, blue, light, dusk, stars, and darkness that one is de-centered, overwhelmed, un-self-consciously absorbed in impossible intensity and raw beauty—one is carried up by a surpassing rhythm of being. This spirituality is radically opposite from that self-centered, "peak-bagging, bragging rights" mentality that has resulted in so many disastrous mountaineering decisions.

In the moment, in the intensity, one's be-ing is so taken up and absorbed in wonder over the surrounding beauty that thought for self is absent. There is a risk here that mountaineers must guard against, for as concern for self dissipates before the wonder of all the surrounding be-ing, one can begin to fail to assess risk-to-self adequately, simply because the significance of one's self has faded to the vanishing point. That is, because of these spiritual dynamics, because of their intrinsic self-forgetfulness, it is easy for mountaineers to be lulled into taking risks—or, more precisely, into not noticing risks—they would never contemplate back home. This absorption into the beauty of the all-encompassing, this de-centering of concern with self, this radical identification with the wonder of the whole can be profoundly comforting. Perhaps this is a source of the oft-praised solace of wilderness experiences: a loss of self-concern that allows one's love for all that is other to become all the more perfect.

Lawrence. For an excellent summary and representative writings, including several late, summary/reflective essays by Naess, see George Sessions, ed., *Deep Ecology for the 21st Century: Readings on the Philosophy and Practice of the New Environmentalism* (Boston: Shambhala Publications, Inc., 1995).

  2. Aldo Leopold, *A Sand County Almanac* (New York: Oxford University Press, 1987), 224–25. For a good introduction to recent discussion of the land ethic, see J. Baird Callicott, *Beyond the Land Ethic: More Essays in Environmental Philosophy* (New York: SUNY Press, 1999).

At the same time, though there is no self-consciousness in view in deep ecological spirituality, it is important to recall that even in the midst of such numinous moments one is not in an utterly self-less state. One wants to live. One strives to live. Indeed, in retrospect it is common for climbers and mountaineers to say that in the throes of such "peak" or "mountaintop experiences" they feel like they are finally, really living, living with an intensity missing in ordinary, day-to-day life.

Perhaps deep ecological theory tends to forget that this spirituality is not utterly self-less because such thoughts come only in retrospect, only when the intensity is lost. Indeed, such thoughts, any thoughts, any active reflection itself signals a break with the lived spiritual intensity, for such un-self-conscious states, such experiences of flow, are also thought-less.[3]

All this describes the non-self-conscious (but not self-less), non-individualistic spirituality of biocentrism. The beauty and wonder of vast and wondrous nature is the overwhelming reality. Significantly, the fundamental spiritual orientation of biocentrism is not utterly inconsistent with the spirituality of our having been seized in and by love for every creature, for deep ecology is characterized by an un-self-conscious, radically inclusive and over-riding concern for all that is other. The other-concern, the love, is common to both biocentrism and to our affirmation of our primordial moral sensitivities and is opposite to the Nietzschean response. For while the Nietzschean recommendation is diametrically opposed to altruism, biocentrism's basic orientation is, in a sense, too radically altruistic.

Whereas the moral spiritual sensitivities I have unveiled and cultivated in this work are fundamentally opposed to the anti-altruistic stance commended by Nietzsche, they are largely continuous with the altruistic, holistic stance commended by biocentrism. However, the spiritual sensitivities I commend are in conflict with the holism of biocentric spirituality, which is radically unselfish but which tends to elide individual Faces. I will, then, offer a qualified affirmation of biocentric spirituality.

INDIVIDUAL FACES AND SYSTEMS

Let me begin by returning to the lion and gazelle example. In principle, biocentrism looks not at that particular lion or that particular gazelle but at that lion's taking of that gazelle in the context of an overall ecosystem.[4] Biocentrism

3. The idea of "flow," named and theorized by Mihaly Csikszentmihalyi, is often utilized in reflections on wilderness experiences and in adventure education. In relation to my appropriation of the concept, precise understanding of the dynamics of flow would have to be adapted to take account of the reality of agape and the dynamics of having been seized in and by love for all creatures.

4. I am focused on unfolding a neo-Levinasian philosophical spirituality in general conversation with the spirituality of Aldo Leopold and of Arne Naess. However, in the technical literature a variety of distinctions are drawn between biocentrism and ecocentrism. In addition to Leopold and

identifies neither with the gazelle nor with the lion but attends to the whole in interrelationship. If the kill is good both for the population of lions and for the population of gazelles, and also for all the other indigenous plants and animals in the ecosystem, then the biocentrist sees not necessary tragedy but a good and healthy event, period. This is in accord with Leopold's famous summary of the land ethic I cited above: "a thing is right when it tends to preserve the integrity, stability, and beauty of the biotic community. It is wrong when it tends otherwise."[5]

Significantly, the biocentric spirituality of the land ethic is profoundly altruistic insofar as it is profoundly non-self-centered. A stark contrast can be drawn here with the amoral, self-centered Nietzschean way of saying "yes" to all that is in the face of this encounter with the lion and the gazelle. Nietzsche recommends denying our classic, moral having been seized for the sake of the ability to affirm our selves and human excellence without compromise. That is, the self-interested, Nietzschean striving for self-affirmation contrasts starkly with the altruistic, wholly holistic spirituality that empowers biocentrism's "yes" to the lion's killing of the gazelle, for the latter turns on a radically non-self-centered, non-selves-centered, ecosystem affirming, biocentric orientation.

Nonetheless, while the path is different, biocentrism no less than Nietzsche calls for us to extirpate our moral sensitivities regarding the violation of other individual creatures. One sees and is concerned with the health and flourishing of the ecosystem, not with the health and flourishing of that particular lion or gazelle.

No doubt the problem with biocentrism can be made most vivid by noting that in theory—though, I should stress, not in the conclusions drawn overtly by biocentrists—*in theory* biocentrism would not make any exception for humans or humanity. That is, there is no reason the holistic vision should suddenly be compromised vis-à-vis humans. Vis-à-vis human actions and any events involving humans, the final and sole deciding evaluative question would be: Do they contribute to the overall health and vibrancy and sustainability of the ecosystem, or do they harm the ecosystem?

From this perspective a notorious comparison between humans as a species—a species that tends to cluster, overpopulate, and quickly lose balance with local ecosystems—and cancer makes some sense. Indeed, from an unqualified, holistic, global perspective, the comparison is apt. Cancer, like humanity, is in and of itself benign. Cancer kills by populating beyond the sustainable capacities of the body until it damages and, if left unchecked, kills its host. And this is indeed akin to the reality of human community not only locally but also in the global ecosystem. When one considers our place near the top of the pyramid of flora and fauna and then puts that together with

Naess, see especially the works of J. Baird Callicott, Val Plumwood, Homes Rolston III, and George Sessions.

5. Aldo Leopold, *A Sand County Almanac,* 224–25.

our tendency to congregate and our exploding numbers, which are already wildly out of ecological balance and evidently destined to continue expanding exponentially until . . . , well, . . . it is possible that our unsustainable expansion, like cancer, will only be halted once we have largely destroyed our host. More precisely, it is possible that our unsustainable expansion on earth will continue until we are brutally beaten back by the consequences of wholesale ecological collapse.

So the comparisons between humanity vis-à-vis the earth's ecosystem on the one hand, and cancer vis-à-vis the body, on the other, are apt. A significant problem with making an objection to biocentrism vivid in this way is that among humans it is likely to provoke an indignant, self-defensive, reactionary response. It is critical not to succumb to this temptation. For not only would that not be a moral reaction, it would reflect and perpetuate the very self-centeredness that has helped to make the cancer comparison all too apt.

We should object to the cancer analogy. Most especially, we should object to the logical inference that just as it is good to kill off the cancer for the sake of the organism, it would be good to kill off humans for the sake of earth's ecosystem. (This has been good fodder for spy thrillers, but mainstream biocentrists are also horrified at the homicidal suggestion.) Nevertheless it is significant that biocentric theory lacks the resources consistently and powerfully to reject the analogy or the homicidal inference. It is critical that the objection to and rejection of this theory be moral, not simply reactionary and self-defensive. And if the objection is moral, then it will be made not only in the name of our fellow human beings but also in the name of that lion and that gazelle.

The *moral* objection to the analogy with cancer, that is, the moral objection to unqualified biocentrism, turns on the way in which biocentrism elides having been seized in and by love for each and every Face. Unqualified biocentrism denies or blinds us to our moral sensitivity to *particular* others, and not only to human others but also, insofar as we are awakened to having been seized in and by love for their Faces, to the pain, despair, and terror of *that* gazelle; for the hunger, need, and satisfaction of *that* lion.

This denial of moral sensitivity to others alerts us to a theoretical problem with biocentrism. There is no reason to think that regional or global ecosystems have any experience of goodness, health, or misfortune. Creatures' bodies evidently form complex, relatively discrete entities that become to varying degrees emergent centers of consciousness, response-ability, and free will, emergent centers of the subjectivity of subjects who can experience joy and sorrow. But there is no evidence that ecosystems become subjects at even the most minimal level.

Even at so simple a level of organization as one finds in an amoeba, it is reasonable to suppose—in accord with continuities one might expect from a nonreductive, nonscientistic evolutionary perspective—that one is encountering a locus of the emergence of a rudimentary subjectivity and capacity to feel. But there is no reason to think that a rainforest, prairie, or mountain names the site of the emergence of a new and unified subject at even such a rudimentary level. The amoeba and all the other creatures in the rainforest or on the mountain to various degrees feel, appreciate, enjoy and suffer. But the mountain does not feel, appreciate, enjoy or suffer at any level. The word "prairie," or the word "mountain," represents a collective, not an emergent complexity, not a locus of subjectivity at even the most primitive level. "Mountain" names a distinct type of geophysical phenomena where one encounters a plurality of subjects. It does not name a subject.

For instance, though one will have to add some qualifiers, it makes literal sense to say that a wolf thinks. While the thinking, loving, fearing, or sorrow of the wolf cannot be equated with the loving, fearing, or sorrow of a human, the findings of evolutionary biology confirm our natural sense that such language describes feelings, emotions, and thoughts of the wolf that are analogous to our own. So, while it makes literal sense to say that a wolf thinks, loves, or fears, it makes no literal sense to say that a mountain thinks, loves, or fears

Talk about mountains thinking, for instance, can be taken seriously, but only with the proviso that the meaning is wholly metaphorical. For there is a distinction between *nonindividuated* systems, collectivities, like mountains, streams, and oceans, on the one hand, and *individuated* systems, bodies, like amoebas and wolves, on the other. Only individuated systems are loci of emergent complexity, the loci, at some level, of subjectivity.

This position is utterly consistent with evolutionary theory. Though you must move beyond a *reductionistic* and/or *scientistic* evolutionism, once you do this you quite reasonably affirm that the joy, love, or anguish of a wolf is not utterly different in kind from our own joy, love, or anguish. Certainly, part of what is going on when the songbird sings has to do with genetic and perhaps even memetic determination, and perhaps also some degree of indeterminacy (i.e., nature, nurture, randomness). But that is also, as we know, the case when we humans sing. Likewise, there is no reason not to think that, in a real if not equivalent sense, the songbird also sings for joy, takes joy in the singing, and when joined by others enjoys the transcending communion that we too enjoy when taken up by the rhythms and beauty of the choir of myriad creatures' chorus.[6]

Even a tree, at a far more radical remove from ourselves, yet still not utterly different in kind, enjoys at least at a cellular level the rays of the sun and the steadying comfort of the nourishing soil that embraces and secures its roots. And here again we have a sense for this thoughtless, cellular level of enjoyment, for we know full well the difference between luxuriating mindlessly in the sun in contrast to *thinking*, "that sun feels good on my skin." That is, even for us the enjoyment is at its most primordial level a nonlinguistic, nonconceptual,

---

6. Charles Hartshorne, working along a discrete but perhaps friendly intellectual trajectory, famously reached a similar conclusion in *Born to Sing: An Interpretation and World Survey of Bird Song* (Bloomington: Indiana University Press, 1992).

cellular event. There is no justification for thinking that one has to be able to *think* in some linguistic form "that sun feels good" to know the warm pleasure. It is not the words that enable the reality but the reality that first inspires and gives substance to the words.[7]

The ability to form concepts and talk gives us many advantages over the tree and enables sorts of enjoyment unavailable to the tree (e.g., the ability to enjoy this text, the ability to enjoy an awareness of the age and character of the sun). Nonetheless, a picture of the ideal beach day hardly involves you, a sea breeze, warm sand, glistening waters, the rhythmic pounding of the waves, and an expert lecturing you on solar physics. To the contrary, on the perfect beach day you strive to realize pure, physical, idea-less, cellular pleasure with the same purity as the tree on the perfect tree day. The idea is to be as much like the tree as possible. You are not concerned with conceptualizing the feeling of the sun's rays but mindlessly, pleasurably soaking them up.

By contrast, we face something different *in kind*, not merely in order of complexity, when we move from the biological to the mineral or elemental, that is, when we move from humans, dolphins, worms, and trees to rocks and H_2O. Across the range of biological organisms we find a graded degree of complexity and similarity of structure, and that makes qualified attribution of analogous capacities reasonable. But we would overstep the bounds of reasonableness if we were to assert that a rock or other such aggregate at any degree of remove experiences something akin to joy, love, or anguish.

In this vein, roughly speaking, process philosophers quite reasonably distinguish *complex entities*, subjects, from *aggregates*, things, on the basis of a distinction in complexity, organization, and unity. A cell, for instance, is a complex entity, functioning in an organized way and in a way obviously akin to all other life—indeed, this may be an analytic statement insofar as we are here broaching one way of distinguishing the living from the nonliving, the animate from the inanimate. By contrast, even the most complicated and intricately formed rock lacks the sort of organized complexity that gives it a new level or integrity of individual being. In other words, the cell is a complex entity and is organized in a dynamic way that results in the emergence of a new and unified level of be-ing, so it is animate, living. A rock, by contrast, may be a complex entity, but it is not organized in such a way that a new kind of unity emerges, so it is inanimate, not living.[8]

7. To speak more technically for a moment, if I were to develop this point I would appropriate distinctions from Heidegger's *Being and Time* (trans. Joan Stambaugh, revised by Dennis Schmidt [Albany, NY: State University of New York Press, 2010]) and contend, speaking now very roughly, that along a continuum the tree enjoys a *situation* (basic, nonconceptual awareness), that the wolf enjoys *a situation* and *understanding* (prelinguistic ability to anticipate, use, and handle creatures and things, concrete but nonreflective understanding), while the human (and in a rudimentary way the wolf) enjoys *a situation, understanding,* and *interpretation* (linguistic, reflective understanding).

8. My approach is very similar to process philosophy and theology, and I could no doubt enter into productive conversation with process thought. However, whereas process thought, inspired by Alfred North Whitehead, developed in the context of English-language, empiricist philosophy, my

What does one do with borderline entities such as viruses? Well, most likely there will always remain borderline cases (this is true with almost any interesting issue), so a first caution is to take care not to allow irresolvable borderline cases to move us to reject more obvious distinctions between the animate and inanimate (e.g., between a rock and an amoeba, let alone between a rock and a horse) about which we have no real doubts. The existence of borderline cases simply tells one where the borders and areas of extant ambiguity lie, no more. They do not render illegitimate those distinctions that can be drawn with confidence. They only caution one about instances where confidence must be appropriately moderated. In general, it would seem to be best to be generous and with regard to the borderline cases we encounter (e.g., viruses) to tilt toward attributing life.

All this helps to make clear a nondefensive, nonanthropocentric, moral objection to biocentrism: biocentrism is morally insufficient in its theoretical articulation to the degree it cannot recognize and articulate our profound sense for the value of subjects. Biocentrism fails to theorize distinctions that allow us to name the discrete, emergent loci of particular others. Biocentrism does not allow us to name and own our having been seized in and by love for discrete others. It does not, for instance, allow us to name or own our conflicted responses and discernment of tragedy in the tale of the lion and the gazelle. Because biocentrism fails to theorize these distinctions and so properly to qualify its claims, it is vulnerable to the comparison between humanity and cancer (with its homicidal, typically anti-environmentalist Hollywood-thriller implications).

Biocentrism's theoretical problem is two-fold. First, biocentrism affirms and celebrates capacities unique to individuals (joy, pain, thinking) while at the same time eliding individuals from view. Second, biocentrism takes these same capacities, capacities indigenous to individuals, and predicates them of nonindividuated collectives (ecosystems), which do not have such capacities.

In other words, in principle an unmitigated deep ecological spirituality values only the ecosystem as a whole. But systems in and of themselves value nothing. Moreover, systems taken whole have no place for value to be concretely realized. Thus the deep ecological perspective is dependent on the moral sensitivities of individual subjects, but it fails to theorize the reality and value of the unique and individual subjects within the reality it values. Generally, then, deep ecological and biocentric spiritualities fail to theorize the value and value-producing reality of living individuals. Individual humans, not humanity, experience delight and are seized by a sense of value (in my neo-Levinasian vocabulary, "are awakened to having been seized by love for Faces"). Horses experience delight and, I would argue, are most likely seized by a sense of value (are awakened). In some rudimentary, concept-less way plants experience delight (e.g., raw, cellular, nonconceptual enjoyment of ideal amounts of sunshine or moisture), though it

---

understanding is inspired by Levinas, whose thought was developed in conversation with Husserl, Heidegger, and predominantly French and German language Continental philosophy, as well as with Russian literature (especially Dostoevsky).

seems far less likely that they are seized by a sense of value. But there is no reason to think that rocks, let alone ecosystems, solar systems, or galaxies, experience delight or value. The value of an ecosystem is no greater than the sum of the awakening/valuing and, derivatively, the value of *subjects*. And since systems do not value, cannot be awakened, there is literally no value in or of the ecosystem qua ecosystem until subjectivity, at however primitive a level, emerges.

Recall my mention of the mountaineer needing to be careful not to be lulled from self-concern so completely that risks are not noticed and mishap, injury, or death soon follow. If the mountaineer is killed, then that spiritual appreciation dies with her. Literally *all* of the spiritual value that the mountaineer's valuing in itself brings into existence dies with her. Since there may be other mountaineers as well as other creatures on the mountain, this is not to say that all value dies with her. But since the value is extant only in relation to some sort of sentience, all the value for which she was the occasion of realization, which she made manifest in her delight and valuing, along with she herself as a creature, an invaluable Face, valued by others in the dynamic that recognizes and manifests and sustains value in the world, all of that vanishes.

To be sure, it is not fantastic to consider that when we recognize a healthy or failing ecosystem we have at some level a vague but not inaccurate sense for the multiple subjectivities at all levels of being that are flourishing or struggling and dying. This, I think, suggests how we can give well-deserved credence to Aldo Leopold when he looks at a mountain and rejoices in the flourishing of the ecosystem, or at the other extreme, when he grieves over a dying mountain. His joy or grief is likely not the result of either a self-centeredness that is reacting solely to the promise or loss of good hunting opportunities, nor is it likely the result of confusedly ascribing subjective capacities to a mountain. It may be best understood in terms of the moral sensitivities of a man highly attuned to and informed about all the creatures of the mountain. It may reflect an inchoate yet accurate sense for all of the suffering and/or all of the delight among a community of subjects extending from the microbiotic to the human. This, I think, is the path along which one can unpack concretely and positively Leopold's famous talk about a mountain thinking (more on this presently). Indeed, this is the path along which one can unpack concretely and positively the moral alertness of biocentric spiritualities generally.

In relation to all of this, it is important to notice the sorts of examples typically used to illustrate and justify various spiritual sensitivities. Consider, for instance, how the story of the lion and the gazelle focuses our attention on individual subjects. By contrast, the stories typically used to convey the spirit of deep ecology focus on high mountain experiences of overwhelming vastness, horizons full of rocky, snow-capped peaks, on distant, fertile landscapes, on the health, wonder, and beauty of whole ecosystems.

Individual animals are too small, too rare, or too distant to seize our attention at this scale. One is taken up and lost in the transcending vastness of mountains, plains, and sky. One sees herds of zebras and gazelles and rivers full of crocs, not the life story of any particular gazelle or crocodile. I think we do indeed discern profound spiritual truths at this more vast scale, and I think the basic spiritual work of awakening, of de-centering, of overcoming our narrow, self-interested ways of being in which nothing looms larger than the concerns and significance of our own selves, is a momentous gift delivered with special power by vast landscapes, bottomless starry skies, and the awe-inspired macro-focus of biocentric spirituality.

The mistake comes when we take spiritual truths discerned on this plane and at this scale and then—with a drive for theoretical closure—articulate an all-encompassing theory that threatens to dominate our understanding in all contexts at every level of attention. At this conceptual juncture—when biocentrism forgets to delimit its claims and where, in particular, it elides the valuing and value of individual others—biocentrism strays logically and morally and renders one less capable of owning and articulating one's having been seized in and by love for each and every creature. As we will consider in the next chapters, this shortcoming is poignantly visible in Aldo Leopold's famous reflection, "Thinking Like a Mountain." Before turning to Leopold, however, let me note why Naess may not only agree with these reflections, but why, despite being largely the founder of the decidedly holistic, biocentric spirituality called "deep ecology," he may also justifiably complain that in my treatment of biocentrism I have missed the nuance of his own position.

In "Self-Realization: An Ecological Approach to Being in the World," which appeared in a collection of essays titled (note the movement from system to individuals), *Thinking Like a Mountain: Towards a Council of All Beings* (emphasis mine), Naess explains that at the core of his thought stands a "process of identification," a "process" that, I believe, attempts to describe the same reality I am striving to describe when I speak of having been seized in and by love for all Faces. Naess explains that his standard example to explain the process of identification has

> to do with a nonhuman being I met forty years ago. I looked through an old-fashioned microscope at the dramatic meeting of two drops of different chemicals. A flea jumped from a lemming strolling along the table and landed in the middle of the acid chemicals. To save it was impossible. It took many minutes for the flea to die. Its movements were dreadfully expressive. What I felt was, naturally, a painful compassion and empathy. But the empathy was *not* basic. What *was* basic was the process of identification, that "I see myself in the flea." If I was alienated from the flea, not seeing intuitively anything resembling myself, the death struggle would have left me indifferent. So there must be identification in order for there to be compassion and, among humans, solidarity.[9]

9. Arne Naess, "Self-Realization: An Ecological Approach to Being in the World," in *Thinking Like a Mountain: Towards a Council of All Beings*, John Seed, Joanna Macy, Pat Fleming, and Arne Naess (Philadelphia: New Society Publishers, 1988), 22.

My neo-Levinasian, quintessentially Christian appeal to having been seized in and by love for the Faces of all faces is starkly different from Naess's appeal to identification. Naess insists that empathy is not basic, that the I's reasoned process of identification is basic ("the empathy was *not* basic. What was basic was the process of identification"). I, by contrast, insist that having been seized in and by love for all Faces is basic (i.e., "primordial"). As a result, while for me the primordial reality empowering the having been seized is an independent and eternally prior reality, namely, the autonomous reality of agape, for Naess the primordial reality is my "intuitive" seeing *of myself* in something other ("I see myself in the flea"). That is, for Naess the primordial reality is a self-regard that is extended when I recognize that something else resembles me. Without that process of seeing myself in the other, I would be indifferent ("If . . . not seeing intuitively anything resembling myself . . . indifferent"). So while for Naess *a process*, the "process of identification," lies at the heart of "compassion and, among humans, solidarity," on my neo-Levinasian, quintessentially Christian understanding, agape is at the heart of compassion and agape is the empowering ground of koinonia (among all beings, each according to its kind).

I believe my neo-Levinasian description of having been seized in and by love for the face of a Face describes more precisely the character of Naess's encounter with the flea, but I still believe that Naess and I are attempting to clothe in language the same primordial spiritual reality. My concern here is biocentric spirituality, however, not Naess per se, so I will not pursue our philosophical differences further. Despite our differences, I think it significant that the father of deep ecology places an encounter with a particular other, a flea, at the heart of his philosophy. In accord with my neo-Levinasian, quintessentially Christian understanding, I would contend that when Naess testifies to the singular event that awakened him to the spiritual heart of deep ecology, he testifies to having been spiritually awakened when he was seized in and by love for the Face of the face of a flea.

Chapter 4

Aldo Leopold and the Wolf

A Confession Betrayed

Aldo Leopold, one of the most revered naturalists of the early twentieth century, was brilliant, sensitive, and incredibly insightful. He saw far beyond the conceptual parameters that impoverished so much twentieth century thought and helped to create a future that could see beyond and critique those blinders. However, he was still a product of and powerfully subject to the creature-negating scientism and anthropocentrism of modern thought. So, unsurprisingly, Leopold's "thinking like a mountain" language is not harmless—not harmless to all the creatures of the mountain and, it is important to note, not harmless to Leopold. Unfortunately, I will argue, distortions inscribed into predominant trajectories of modern Western rationality led Leopold to betray in his articulated understanding a dimension of his own most profound moral sensitivities.

Leopold unintentionally but explicitly signals his subservience to creature-negating conceptual trajectories in his famous essay, "Thinking Like a Mountain." Leopold begins the essay with what he describes as the "sorrow" discernible in the wild howl of a wolf. His second paragraph begins with the "heed" that "every living thing" pays to that call: the "reminder" to the deer, the "forecast" to the pine, the "promise" for the coyote, the "threat" and "challenge" to the "cowman" and hunter.[1] But, instead of refining and continuing with this sort of attention to multiple subjectivities, Leopold turns to the "deeper" understanding of the mountain, which alone is able to "listen *objectively*" (objectivity being a prime value for modern Western rationality).[2]

When he immediately goes on to describe this "objective" knowledge, however, Leopold returns to descriptions of the reactions of various creatures for whom the cry of the wolf brings "tingles in the spine."[3] In this unqualified oscillation between things like mountains and subjects like deer and coyote one discerns a biocentric eliding of individuals that immediately betrays Leopold, alienating him from his own most profound moral sensitivities.

In one of the most famous passages in all of his writings, the next story Leopold shares in the essay is the life-altering event that first led him to "think like a mountain." He and his party were sitting on the rim of a canyon eating lunch when they saw what they thought was a doe fording the stream far below. They realized their error when the wolf emerged from the water and shook out her coat, at which point six other wolves, "evidently grown pups, sprang from the willows and all joined in a welcoming melee of wagging tails and playful maulings. What was literally a pile of wolves writhed and tumbled in the center of an open flat at the foot of our rimrock."[4]

"In a second," Leopold writes, "we were pumping lead into the pack." Leopold says they shot more with excitement than with accuracy. When the gunfire died the mother wolf was down and "a pup was dragging a leg into impassable slide-rocks."[5] "We reached the old wolf," Leopold says, "in time to watch a fierce green fire dying in her eyes." "I realized then, and have known ever since," he says, "that there was something new to me in those eyes—something known only to her and to the mountain."[6]

And then he offers this abortive apology and confession, "I was young then, and full of trigger-itch; I thought that because fewer wolves meant more deer, that no wolves would mean hunters' paradise. But after seeing the green fire die, I sensed that neither the wolf nor the mountain agreed with such a view."[7]

Note how at the close of this paragraph the subjectivity of the wolf has subtly been equated with the "subjectivity" of the mountain, and thereby negated. By the time Leopold reaches his closing paragraphs in this part of the essay, the perspective of the wolf has been wholly absorbed into the "objective" perspective of the mountain. His analysis turns to later experiences where he has witnessed how the eradication of wolves leads to overpopulation of deer, which leads to decimation of the mountain ecosystem, which leads to a crash in the deer

1. Aldo Leopold, *A Sand County Almanac* (New York: Oxford University Press, 1987), 129.
2. Ibid; emphasis mine.
3. Ibid.
4. Ibid., 130.
5. Ibid.
6. Ibid.
7. Ibid.

population. Before long the category-confusions dominate Leopold's prose. Subjects (e.g., deer) are simply equated with nonindividuated systems or groups (e.g., deer *herds*, mountains). The "deer *herd* lives in mortal fear of its wolves," says Leopold, just as mountains "live in mortal fear" of their deer.[8] Obviously, in contrast to individual deer, however, neither a herd nor a mountain "fears," "hungers," or does anything else that subjects do.

At the close of the reflection Leopold returns to talk of individual deer and humans, but then he falls immediately (perhaps strategically) into describing the ultimate lesson in terms of human self-interest: we all desire peace in our time, but in removing from the ecosystem all that seems to threaten us, such as the wolf, we may, unwittingly but ultimately, be destroying ourselves. The "objective" viewpoint of the mountain and the threat posed to deer by the eradication of predators suggests that too much peace may be a dangerous thing, the "objective" viewpoint suggests that, in this sense, preserving an enduring degree of threat and otherness within the world is essential to achieving maximal peace in our time and in the time of our grandchildren. This, Leopold suggests (I think mistakenly), may have been the meaning of Thoreau's dictum, "In wildness is the salvation of the world."[9] Thoreau was anthropocentric, but I nonetheless suspect that he had a far more spiritual meaning in mind than is suggested by Leopold's "objective" (and radically anthropocentric) appeal.

The reason I think Leopold's own moral sensitivities are betrayed (rather than simply lacking) in this famous reflection on thinking like a mountain has to do with the sympathy and power and apology rendered in his account of the killing of the wolves. Leopold writes with such economy and grace, and his writing is so disciplined by his rigor as the dispassionate, observational scientist, that his most profound passages are never calculated for emotional impact. Nonetheless, Leopold's narrative of the wolf with her burning green eyes is both damning and profoundly saddening.

Imagine the scene. The young wolves have remained in hiding, hoping for the safe return of their mother. Even as they see her fording the creek, they remain in safe hiding, bursting out of the willows in glee only after their mother has fully returned. No doubt the mother is relieved not only at making it back safely but at finding her cubs safe. And then there is the wondrous greeting and play, all the tension and anxiety of separation melts away. Pure abandon and joy. Tossing and rolling and nipping and playing. The mother and brothers and sisters piling in together. Then bang, bang, bang. Lead whistles past, dull thuds of impact, crack of shattering bones, howls of pain, agony. The joyous

8. Ibid., 132.
9. Ibid., 133. Thoreau's quote, which Leopold paraphrases from *Walking*, reads in full, "The West of which I speak is but another name for the Wild; and what I have been preparing to say is, that in Wildness is the preservation of the World. Every tree sends its fibers forth in search of the Wild. The cities import it at any price" (Henry David Thoreau, *Walking* [Rockville, MD: Arc Manor, 2007], 26).

moment broken forever. A dying pup dragging himself away. A helpless mother. Paralyzed. Dying. Joy rent. Utter despair. Finality. Evil.

And then appears the face of your and your children's murderer. You had been playing with your children, had heard their squeals of glee turn into screams of pain and horror, and then the face of one of the murderers, "full of trigger itch," is looking down into your eyes. You cannot speak, but your green eyes burn with accusation, devastation: "Why?" "What sort of evil are you?"

Certainly that wolf lacked the words and concepts to speak or think as do we. But words are only the barest attempt to communicate abstractly the reality that they signify, a reality that is known bodily, a primordial having been seized by love that screams *no* to all the horror and evil. Words are abstract gestures urging us toward the significant reality they invoke. The truly significant reality behind the look of those green eyes was not *words*.[10]

That wolf knew none of my words. She did not reflect verbally as I do. But she knew the realities, the reality of nursing cubs grown strong, of separation and return, of play, joy, peace, and contentment, and now of horror and violation-to-death for her and her cubs and their love. That, and now I am not speaking metaphorically, is the clear accusation presented by the fire in those dying green eyes—*not* some unspecified "objective" knowledge shared by the wolf and the mountain.

Leopold protects himself, evades the accusation hurled at him from behind those burning green eyes, when he puts the "objective" thoughts of the mountain behind those eyes, when he moves oh-so-rapidly to biocentrism. He is to be commended for the honesty with which he recounted the event, which had evidently haunted him for the decades since his youth. This haunting is not surprising. Partly due to the spiritual betrayal inscribed within the modern mentality within which he had been formed, one expects that Leopold would have continued to be haunted by this horror. Forgiveness of oneself cannot exceed the fullness of one's confession. And the fullness of this evil act remained yet to be fully confessed. In this sense Leopold himself was betrayed, prevented from fully articulating his guilt and so prevented from full repentance, which in turn prevented him from finding grace (for reasons detailed below), prevented him from finding himself expiated, prevented him from being able to see and affirm, eyes wide open to evil, eyes wide open to his complicity and culpability, a "yes" to himself.

Given his guilt over this youthful incident, which still clearly haunts him at the end of his life (the essay is found in *A Sand County Almanac*, which Leopold completed shortly before his death in 1948, at age sixty-one), it would be understandable if Leopold were tempted in part by a comfort one might gain from biocentrism that is subtle and superficially attractive but illegitimate.

---

10. I have in mind something like the prelinguistic "understanding" Heidegger unfolds at length in *Being and Time*, the general outline of which is visible when he says, "Knowing is a mode of Dasein which is founded in being-in-the-world. Thus, being-in-the-world, as a fundamental constitution, requires a *prior* interpretation" (Heidegger, *Being and Time*, [trans. Joan Stambaugh, revised by Dennis Schmidt (Albany, NY: State University of New York Press, 2010)], 62.).

Biocentrism's eliding of concern for individuals illicitly protects us from naming and opening ourselves fully to the overwhelming pain that surrounds us. In fact every ecosystem does, and shy of some miracle forever will depend on violence, killing, and consumption. To the degree biocentrism allows denial of this, it is attractive because it is escapist. While biocentrism is right to remind us that the lion killing the gazelle is a necessary part of a healthy ecosystem and so is, in terms of the ecosystem and the overall benefit of all its subjects, a relative good, a moral perspective can never affirm it as sheer good, for the moral perspective never forgets the pain, fear, and loss of that gazelle.

With that in mind, one drops talk of "good" and begins speaking of "necessary evil" and of the *tragic* character of existence (it is no accident that Nietzsche rejects this classic understanding of the "tragic"). Biocentrism can be tempting, then, insofar as its unqualified holism can help us deny the degree to which reality devastatingly fails to live up to our most profound hopes for the good. But this is a temptation that a moral perspective can no more abide in biocentrism than in Nietzschean transvaluation.

As Leopold's haunting moral sensitivity to the wolf illustrates, advocates of biocentrism are not moral monsters. They are repulsed by the analogy that compares humans to cancer and would be horrified by any suggestion that we should kill people in order to save the ecosystem. This suggests that moral awakening to Faces, even if it is inadequately theorized, remains in play in the spirituality of deep ecological and land ethic advocates. Thus, in contrast to Nietzsche, biocentrism cannot say an unmitigated "yes" to all that is even within a healthy ecosystem, for moral concern for every individual remains surreptitiously in play within biocentric spiritualities. That is, for biocentrism as well as for traditional morality, the spiritual problem of evil, a felt need to meet the challenge to legitimate affirmation of oneself and the world amid all the pain, suffering, and injustice (i.e., survivor guilt) should remain in play.

Aldo Leopold's use of the story of the wolves in order to foster biocentrism is revealing for the very reason it is rare: namely, because of the centrality not only of a mountain but also of individuals to the story. The centrality of ecosystems— mountains, oceans, rivers, forests, plains—in biocentrism is paradigmatic and entirely understandable. When attention is drawn to ecosystems or animal groups (e.g., herds of deer, flocks of geese) particular others are not in view, so the competing spiritual emphases that are brought into play in, for instance, the story of the lion and gazelle are never raised. But as we have seen, if the focus on vast landscapes like mountains is not immediately qualified by attention to the significance of individuals, then biocentrism becomes not only illogical (i.e., insofar as value in biocentrism is parasitic on moral valuations essentially related to precisely the individuals elided from view) but also immoral (insofar as it is helpless before the humanity-is-like-cancer example or, to the other extreme, facilitates the denial of the value and valuing of nonhuman animals, as illustrated vis-à-vis Leopold).

Deep ecological spirituality can be celebrated, then, but only if one remembers that it applies only within very specific and strictly delimited contexts. That is, the spirituality depends on a rarified context and becomes immoral and escapist the moment it is maintained despite the appearance of the Faces of particular others within one's horizon. I have no doubt that Leopold and Naess, and quite possibly all biocentric theorists, would concur with this assertion. The problem is rooted, I suspect, in an overreaction to the anthropocentrism of much twentieth century environmentalism, which resulted in a theoretical overcompensation that tilted too far in a holistic direction. The problem, then, is contextual and theoretical. Significantly, the problem does not lie in the profound spirituality that shines through in both Leopold and Naess's works.

We can be sure, as noted, that even if Leopold or, most especially, Naess (remember the flea) were deep into the wilderness, high up on a beautiful, barren peak, or lost in the wonder of some majestic whole, the value of an individual would rush into focus the second a companion was injured. And now above all they would be fighting to get her off the mountain and to save her life. At such junctures the subterranean but absolute having been seized in and by love for every Face that lies at the root of biocentrism would become manifest in the care, worry, effort, and sacrifice made for one subject. Because of this same subterranean but profound love for every Face, the cold-blooded analogy that compares humanity to cancer, along with its homicidal implications, has always been morally horrifying to deep ecologists and advocates of the land ethic.

The tragic error toward which biocentrism (including its manifestation vis-à-vis deep ecology or the land ethic) has a *theoretical* tendency, namely, the tendency to forget one's having been seized in and by love for individual others (and indirectly for oneself), must be acknowledged if, as I have argued, one is to prevent the emergence of an unqualified holism that results in an illogical and immoral spirituality. There is every reason to expect that all biocentrists, and most certainly Leopold and Naess, would immediately acknowledge this problem. Moreover, the self-forgetfulness, other-centeredness, and radical awakening to every Face (the Face of the wolf, the lion, the gazelle, even the flea) that characterizes biocentric spirituality is a profound manifestation of agape in the classic sense of "selfless love" or, in my neo-Levinasian formulation, "having been seized in and by love for all Faces." Because of this stark ambiguity, even as I criticize a very problematic tendency of biocentric spirituality, I celebrate and affirm central aspects of biocentric spirituality. Moreover, I affirm and, especially for those who are emotionally wounded, recommend the long acknowledged and rightly treasured ability of wilderness sojourns to bring healing, solace, peace, and even joy.

In these first four chapters I have unfolded and disarmed three powerful modern Western evasions of the spiritual challenge of evil. First, and most familiar, I considered righteous rejection of God, which is typically a loving reaction to the intense pain and suffering of others. I argued, in the spirit of the psalms of lament, that this reaction is in a certain sense both understandable and admirable. I worked to affirm the need to work sympathetically with and even to accommodate this reaction. After rejecting God, however, we are left with precisely all the same evil, at which point the accusation hurled against God redounds back against us, others, and the world. So morally indignant rejection of God is ultimately futile against the spiritual challenge of affirming ourselves, others, and the world in the face of evil.

Second, I described a conceptual move especially common among modern Western intellectual elites, the widespread Nietzschean transvaluation (i.e., wholesale eliding) of values. On Nietzschean and neo-Nietzschean understanding, there is in fact no moral reality—this is the significance of the death of God in Nietzsche's thought. There is only existence as brute fact and our preferences. Traditional values carried by religious and cultural traditions are not a reflection of moral reality. They are wholly a product of evolutionary and sociocultural forces. Since there is no moral reality, there is no legitimate imperative to abide by any moral values. Worse yet, as Nietzsche realized, traditional ideas of good and evil deliver condemnation of ourselves and the world. So Nietzsche recommended we extirpate our moral sensitivities. That is, he recommended we move beyond the very idea of the moral, beyond the very idea of good and evil. Thereby we are freed from all accusation. Nietzsche's denial of moral reality, however, is not established by any philosophical argument and is grossly counterintuitive. Moreover, it facilitates exploitation. So Nietzsche's position is both philosophically weak and ethically dangerous.

Finally, I addressed the unwitting eliding of Faces in biocentric understanding, as illustrated in Leopold's land ethic and Naess's deep ecology. In this case, the problem is almost wholly theoretical, for there is ample reason to expect that advocates of the land ethic and of deep ecology, like Leopold and Naess themselves, have indeed been seized in and by love for individual creatures. Once this theoretical lacuna has been named, the three-fold spiritual challenge of affirmation in the face of evil (affirmation of ourselves, of others, and of the world) is manifest.

In the wake of the displacement of these three evasions, the single question this spiritual exploration strives to address is all the more clearly manifest. *How*, once we confront the spiritual challenge of affirmation of ourselves, others, and the world while facing squarely the reality of evil, *how*, once we move beyond all evasions, once we realize that all the passionate protest so often screamed out against God must be turned against reality itself and against ourselves insofar as we are part and parcel of that reality, how are we, eyes wide open in this vale of tears, not consumed by guilt and grief? *How* are we not overcome by survivor guilt? *How* are we to avoid both horns of the dilemma of mutilation (i.e., how are we to avoid both spiritual condemnation and spiritual mutilation)? Moving past the influential modern Western forms of evasion considered in these opening chapters, living awakened, eyes wide open to all the pain, suffering, and injustice suffusing reality, we are returned all the more forcefully to the spiritual challenge of affirmation in the face of evil.

I believe the saving answer to the spiritual challenge of evil lies at the heart of Jewish and Christian spirituality (among others): namely, the saving answer lies in the reality of agape, in the dynamics of having been seized in and by love for all Faces, dynamics that give us a wholly reasonable, primordial, and ultimate affirmation of our world, of others, and of ourselves—dynamics that legitimate moments when we revel in pure joy—all without in any way evading, denying, or looking away from all the enduring pain, suffering, and injustice suffusing the world.

PART 2
AGAPE AND THE
PARADISE OF "YES"

Chapter 5

Concerning Reality

Primordially and Ultimately, "Yes"

THE THREEFOLD SPIRITUAL CHALLENGE OF EVIL

Once we awaken and open ourselves wholly to all the Faces that surround us, the spiritual challenge of evil emerges not from lack of meaning—we have moved definitively beyond modernity's morally barren "quest for meaning"—and of course not from joy over happy Faces or the glory of mutually awakened, Face-to-Face communion. The spiritual challenge of evil emerges from having been seized in and by love for Faces afflicted by pain, suffering, and injustice. In retrospect, we realize how the evasions of modernity mask the devastating and seemingly insurmountable spiritual challenge of evil, a challenge that continually afflicts all who are morally awake in this world, a world suffused with evil.

The spiritual challenge of affirmation in the face of evil is threefold. First, can we say a primordial and ultimate "yes" to reality? Second and third, given that we are inextricably embedded within and so inextricably bound up with this world and are ourselves guilty of causing harm, can we hear and say an eyes wide open, primordial and ultimate "yes" to others and to ourselves? I am now in a position to try to make clear why the answer to the threefold challenge of affirmation is a wholehearted and sure, if precisely qualified, "yes." For the dynamics of what I will identify as a decisive asymmetry, the dynamics of having been seized in and by love for all Faces, along with the transcending joy of mutually awakened Face-to-Face communion, all taken together, allow us— without denial and utterly reasonably—to accept, celebrate, and proclaim the primordial and ultimate gift of "yes" to reality and to ourselves.

Let me digress momentarily and make sure that a basic point about the character of this exploration is clear. I will not be inferring or establishing the spiritual truth of this "yes" through argument in the modern, foundationalist (let alone empiricist) sense. It will not be the case that after rigorous reflection I will conclude we can validly infer "yes" to existence, others, and ourselves, as if we are at base stepping back conceptually, reasoning, and then dispassionately drawing some conclusion about existence. It is rather that rigorous reflection helps awaken us to a "yes," rigorous reflection helps us to understand, to realize consciously and more fully to inhabit, embrace, and celebrate a "yes" that is primordial and ultimate, a "yes" that is always already given to all Faces, a "yes" that is always already indirectly but decisively given to each of us.

To be sure, the "yes" will be qualified, for evil is real and enduring. We ever have and, shy of some literal and radical divine intervention, we ever will live and die amidst enduring evil in this vale of tears. Our wholehearted "yes" will be qualified by the enduring reality of pain, suffering, and injustice, by the enduring reality of all to which we say a passionate "no." But we can understand how suffering, evil, injustice, and our passionate "no" are nevertheless not primordial and ultimate, not alpha and omega, not wholly devastating. As inspired most especially by Emmanuel Levinas, in these two chapters I will strive to explain how, wholly reasonably and eyes wide open to evil, we can accept, affirm, and celebrate an always already given, primordial and ultimate "yes" to reality, to others, and to ourselves.

AGAPE, ASYMMETRY, AND AFFIRMATION

A first step in realizing how we can accept, celebrate, and affirm an always already given primordial and ultimate "yes" to reality and to ourselves lies in the recognition that *our reaction to good and evil is impassioned and asymmetrical.* Insofar as we are awakened, we are fundamentally response-able and alive to having been seized in and by love for the Faces of others. When Faces are blessed with love, joy, flourishing, harmony, and happiness, we rejoice. When Faces are afflicted by despair, suffering, strife, and sorrow, we cry out in pain and protest. To the degree we do not close our eyes or harden our hearts, we find ourselves always already desiring good, abhorring evil, and moved to action. Having been seized in and by love for the Faces of others, we are immediately moved to work for good and to resist evil.[1]

---

1. In chapter 8, "A Knowing Idealism: The Decisive Asymmetry," in *For the Love of All Creatures: The Story of Grace in Genesis*, I unfold the decisive asymmetry in conversation with the primeval history of Genesis ([Grand Rapids: William B. Eerdmans Publishing Co., 2015], 125–41).

Let me be perfectly clear about a basic contention: having been seized in and by love for the Faces of others is a most basic, self-evident, undeniable (in that sense solid, objective) and significant manifestation of reality. There is nothing more real and significant than love and, derivatively, its violation (i.e., evil).

All of this leads to two pivotal, primordially and ultimately affirming realizations. First, spiritually, which is to say, as Faces, we are seized in and by love. Moreover, as I will strive to make clear, insofar as we live awakened to having been seized in and by love, that is, insofar as we live in and by faith, we find ourselves primordially and ultimately affirmed by an amazing grace.

Second, insofar as our having been seized in and by love for all Faces is not a product of any decision or act of will on our part, but is an always already prior, primordial and ultimate having been seized, we realize that love does not originate in us. Love is that in and by which we always already find ourselves seized. Love is a nonphysical but objective/autonomous reality in which, primordially and ultimately, we live and move and have our being.

Moreover, while in the face of great evil and injustice all are vulnerable to finding themselves consumed by hatred and evil, we can realize that we do not fundamentally embrace and affirm evil. To the contrary, absent debilitating trauma or conscious hardening of our hearts, we celebrate, affirm, and live into having been seized in and by love for the Faces of all others, and as a result we mourn, protest, and resist violation of good (i.e., evil). All of this names a decisive asymmetry. Love is primordial and ultimate. "Evil"/"no!" is derivative and secondary. For it does not name an independent reality. It names the violation of "yes," the violation of a Face. In the language traditionally used to name and make this reality manifest in the sphere of language and reason, we can realize that love is primordial and ultimate (i.e., that love is divine, that love is God, that God is love), and, to repeat, we realize that this is a most basic, self-evident, undeniable, and significant manifestation of reality.[2]

RECLAIMING MORAL REALISM/IDEALISM
IN THE CLASSIC/TRADITIONAL SENSE

Our reaction to the story of the lion and gazelle involves all the spiritual dynamics I am striving to unfold. We name as real the Faces of the lion and of the gazelle. That is, we name as an irreducible aspect of reality our having been seized in and by love for the lion and our having been seized in and by love for the gazelle. In our concern for the desperate and fleeing gazelle we manifested an absolutely prior and irreducibly real having been seized. We now realize that, true to the spirit of our most primordial having been seized, and contrary to common modern Western philosophical misconception, authentic valuing

2. While I cannot defend the claim here (for lack of space and expertise), I suspect that in diverse but commensurable ways a multitude of faith traditions describe this same reality.

is not rooted in self-conscious and autonomous decision making. We do not *initiate* our valuing of the gazelle or lion. We do not first *decide* the gazelle or lion has moral worth. We do not begin by *calculating* the gazelle or lion's worth. We do not parcel out our sadness over the gazelle's death or our joy over the lion's success in her hunt in accord with a distinct and dispassionately developed scale of value. Insofar as our hearts are not hardened we find ourselves having been seized in and by love for the Faces of the lion *and* of the gazelle.

Moreover, in our "no"/"yes" to the gazelle's death and to the lion's receiving of essential sustenance, we undergo in fullness each aspect of the decisive asymmetry. In the tragic tale of the lion and the gazelle we find in microcosm the essential dynamics of life lived awake, eyes wide open in this vale of tears: joy over the lion's success in the hunt (i.e., "yes"), horror over the killing of the gazelle (i.e., "no"), the tragic character of a carnivorous world (i.e., "yes"/"no"), and the decisive asymmetry that reveals that "yes" is primordial and ultimate (i.e., the realization of the power/reality of the "yes" of the having been seized and the realization that every "no" is a "yes-violated").

FOCUSED ATTENTION AND INNOCENT JOY

As we review the essential character of each of these moments, we should explicitly note a significant characteristic of human attention: To the degree our attention is seized it becomes focused. As our attention becomes focused it becomes delimited. The more intensely it is seized, the more delimited its focus. On reflection, of course, we can unfold and affirm the complexities even of intensely delimited attention. We can grant not only the obvious point that the ethical complexity of any moment may exceed the singularity that delimits highly focused attention, we can grant that at some level of consciousness (or of un- or sub-consciousness, or some such) those complexities may well be affecting the character of our attention and overall sensibilities. These qualifications in hand, we can still note that in any given moment of focused attention, multiplicity and complexity give way to singularity.

For instance, as our attention is concentrated in the moment of having been seized in and by love for the Face of the gazelle, all else momentarily slides from notice. But then as the camera pans to the tall grass and focuses in on the ears and eyes of the lion in the background our focused attention is taken in sequence by the "no" (i.e., to the gazelles' plight), perhaps by a "yes" to the gazelles' impossibly quick bursting into flight, and then, with the lion's isolation of the slowest gazelle and the kill, by either "no" (for the gazelle) or "yes" (for the lion and her cubs). We cannot attend simultaneously to both the "yes" and "no" of the "yes"/"no" (i.e., to the "no-for-gazelle," which is simultaneously "yes-for-lion"), for in the moment we only live into either the "yes" or the "no." Only on reflection can we acknowledge the complexity and name the tragic character of the necessity that brings a "yes" that will simultaneously be a "no," or recognize the decisive asymmetry: namely, that ultimately a "yes" stands behind, engenders, and fires passion into every "no."

Because of the focused character of concentrated attention, in relatively discrete and happy contexts (the wedding, the birthing room), in moments when we are wholly taken up by "yes" we can live in blissful ignorance of the evil suffusing reality. In such transcending moments we forget all else. Explicit consciousness even of our very own selves fades to nothing. We conceive of our presence only indirectly and after-the-fact, on reflection. In the grip of the moment our attention is wholly and gloriously taken up in joy for the other, in the gift of the having been seized. The good we are celebrating is not ethical but wholly moral and aesthetic, and so there is no shadow of evil in our consciousness, nor should there be. In order to clarify the distinctions I am drawing here among moral, aesthetic, and ethical good, let me cite a passage from *For the Love of All Creatures: The Story of Grace in Genesis*, where I unfold the distinctions in detail:

> It does not follow, however, that if one is to have good in *any* sense that one must have evil, for we can distinguish two senses of good that are meaningful in the absence of any evil. First, there is good in the sense of the transcending joy of having been seized by love for others, that is, what we will call good in a *moral* sense ("moral" because it is other-responsive, but not yet "ethical" because there is no yes-violated). I do not need any concept of evil in order to enjoy and conceive of the good of having been seized by love for others (*agape*). Second, there is good in the sense of delight (i.e., love in the sense of eros) in some creature or thing, for instance, in a symphony, a rainbow, a fresh-picked bowl of strawberries, or the body of a lover — that is, good in an *aesthetic* sense. And again, there is good in . . . the sense in which we judge resistance to injustice or suffering to be good, good in contrast to evil, good in contrast to "yes-violated," good in an *ethical* sense.[3]

In moments when our attention is wholly captured by what is morally and aesthetically good and/or beautiful, we are not denying or looking away from evil. We are not evading the reality of evil, we are not consciously denying that at that very moment horrors are filling other places, we are not consciously denying that at other times horrors have filled this place, this place where we are now wholly and gloriously caught up by a vision of goodness and/or beauty. But while we do not deny or consciously look away from the realities of evil, we nevertheless enjoy the delimited, discrete, finite character of intensely focused attention. Without denial, hard-heartedness, or evasion, then, when caught up in transcending moments of goodness and beauty we innocently celebrate and luxuriate in pure joy.

Even here in this vale of tears, then, we can know glorious, precious, innocent moments when we are wholly taken up by the surpassing purity and power of "yes," moments of intensely focused attention when we find ourselves having been seized in and by love for the Faces of others in joyous circumstances. In

---

3. Greenway, *For the Love of All Creatures*, 133.

such moments of sheer and unadulterated joy, all the evil and ambiguity fade to nothing—not because of any evasion or self-protective looking away, not out of an attempt to deny complicity and culpability, not as part of any assertion of personal dessert (i.e., not because I deserve to be joyful), not because I can claim a right to be, that is, a right to "my place in the sun," but because abandoning all hope of claiming any right to be, abandoning all hope of establishing the righteousness of our be-ing, abandoning every attempt to save ourselves, we surrender ourselves, lose ourselves to agape and on such wondrous occasions lose ourselves to moments of intensely focused, wholly joyful, narrowly delimited attention to the gift of having been seized in and by the love for a Face.[4]

For example, our focused attention may be wholly taken up in having been seized in and by love for the Face of a precious friend, a child, a grandchild, a horse, cat, dog, perhaps a wild gazelle or lion, or even a flea. In some cases, we may glory in that transcending, *mutually awakened* communion that is realized when one is seized in and by love for a Face who is awake and seized in and by love for our own Face. Not only can we be taken up in moments of pure joy with and for others, we can be taken up in moments of sheer aesthetic delight. All the evil and ambiguity can momentarily fade to nothing as we are wholly taken up in the beauty of a glorious sunset, a vibrant rainbow, blue mountain vistas, or the exquisite vibrato of a violin. Such innocent moments of sheer moral or aesthetic bliss are surely rare and fleeting, but we rightly number them among the most profound, true, life-giving, and precious moments in our lives.

THE PARADOX OF EVIL AND THE CONVICTION OF "YES"

While we rightly take joy and sustenance from wholly good and happy events, the death of the gazelle that is simultaneously the necessary feeding of the lion and her cubs makes clear the tragic character of life in this world. Affirmation of reality would lack integrity and resilience if it were to be derived wholly or even primarily from good and joyful occasions, for in that case affirmation would depend on evasion. Moreover, I would have no right to my repeated invocation of "innocence" if, with regard to reality and life, I had to conclude with a primordial and ultimate "it's no good." That is why recognition of the decisive asymmetry, of the "yes" behind and empowering every "no," is so significant. Indeed, that is why it is so significant that recognition of the decisive asymmetry can be most profoundly and powerfully manifest in the face of the greatest horrors.

It is common but mistaken to conclude that evil poses the greatest threat to the affirmation that love is primordial and ultimate. In fact, once the dynamics of the decisive asymmetry are discerned, one recognizes that precisely in the face

4. Blaise Pascal, *Pensées*, trans. A. J. Krailsheimer (New York: Penguin Books, 1966), 47—*la pensée* 64 in Kraislheimer and *la pensée* 295 in the Brunschvicg edition.

of the most profound evils the recognition of agape as primordial and ultimate can dawn with the fullest power and resilience.

Admittedly, this connection between evil and recognition that love is primordial and ultimate sounds paradoxical. But at one level the point is obvious, for it is commonly recognized that our passion for what is right and good rises up with unparalleled force and even righteous ferocity precisely when we are confronted with intense evil (e.g., an evil so overwhelming and potent it leads to impassioned rejection of God).

Inspiration regarding the reality of having been seized in and by love for Faces flows as much from pain and sorrow as from joy and happiness, as much from "no" as from "yes." So it is most true and accurate to understand the undeniable, wrenching, having been seized that calls forth our impassioned, ethical "no" in terms of an intense "yes-violated" (i.e., in terms of the decisive asymmetry). Paradoxically but surely, the more intense our offense over evil, the more impassioned is our lived awakening to the reality of the having been seized, to the realization that "yes" is primordial and ultimate.

In this sense it is not surprising that Emmanuel Levinas, whose understanding was refined in the fires of the Holocaust, is the figure who above all inspires this exploration.[5] This is because the critical, vital, hopeful, life-giving recognition, recognition of the decisive asymmetry, flows from precise realization of the dynamics of pain and sorrow, from recognition of our foundational and unshakable sense of what *should be*, from a sense for well-being that is awfully violated, from realization of the "yes" firing the passion in every "no." This names the recognition of the decisive asymmetry that makes clear that *yes*, agape, is alpha and omega. It is this dynamic that will allow for qualified, primordial, and ultimate affirmation of existence even as our eyes remain wide open to enduring evil. Let me be the first to concede, however, that on occasion an injury or horror can be so extreme that it becomes physically (e.g. brain injury) or psychologically debilitating. Indeed, the possibility of such pain and horror is so significant that I will now digress in order very deliberately and explicitly to name its potentially debilitating power.

---

5. For details on Levinas' life see "Interview with François Poirié," in Emmanuel Levinas, *Is It Righteous to Be? Interviews with Emmanuel Levinas*, ed. Jill Robbins (Stanford: Stanford University Press, 2001), 23–83; as well as *The Cambridge Companion to Levinas*, ed. Simon Critchley and Robert Bernasconi (Cambridge: Cambridge University Press, 2002), xix–xx; and also Salomon Malka, *Emmanuel Levinas: His Life and Legacy*, trans. Michael Kigel and Sonja M. Embree (Pittsburgh: Duquesne University Press, 2006). Though his influence has so far remained largely in the background—I consider his work in detail below—I should also mention the life of Fyodor Dostoevsky, whose final work, *The Brothers Karamazov*, decisively influenced Levinas (and this exploration). As a young man Dostoevsky was a political prisoner who was tried, convicted of capital treason, and imprisoned. On the morning of his scheduled execution he was marched to the post to which he would be tied and shot, and only then was a decree from the Czar read that reduced his sentence to several more years in prison. Also possibly pertinent, Dostoevsky penned this final work shortly after the death of his beloved little girl.

DEBILITATING PAIN AND HORROR

I have been determined to attend to the most concrete, real, powerful and profound dimensions of life: to love, to the good, to the beautiful, and to evil. Lest my delineating of the asymmetry inadvertently perpetuates any measure of a Pollyannaish mentality, however, let me hasten to affirm that it is critical to remain utterly realistic about the physical and psychological realities of life in this vale of tears. Not only may any of us at any time suffer a debilitating brain injury, but we can imagine other traumas so intimate and horrible they become overwhelming, especially when such tragedy crushes Faces precious to us (e.g., our children, parents, siblings). We are all vulnerable. Anyone may have their brain physically altered (e.g., in an automobile accident) or be rendered emotionally inconsolable by an overwhelming horror. Nothing I am saying gainsays the importance of pastoral or other professional counseling, medical intervention, or the critical role of loving support from family and friends.

Moreover, I am most certainly not contending that this understanding makes everything "OK" in the face of trauma. While I have rejected as unrealistic and dishonest any explicit attempt to "transvalue" our values and/or to deny the reality of evil, I acknowledge that lashing out at God is an understandable response to overwhelming loss. The Hebrew psalms of lament are full of bitter accusations and questions directed at God. The psalmists understand that when we are overcome by incomprehensible evil and/or injustice, hurling bromides at a deity who is thought to have the power simply to change the course of events is, psychologically speaking, utterly natural and understandable (and deserving of sympathetic response). But I have also explained why lashing out at God fails, ultimately, to provide healing or comfort and so finally proves futile and unhelpful, and how it can even facilitate denial and evasion.

To be sure, vis-à-vis the *logical* problem of evil, if there actually exists a deity who could have intervened in order to prevent the horrors of the world, then that deity has, to put it mildly, some serious explaining to do. Given our understanding of the ultimate and primordial character of love, if such a deity does "exist" (and affirmation of the reality of such a personal, agential deity is not inconsistent with this exploration, though it lies beyond its parameters), we would expect some good answer to come eventually. But I do not know what that answer might be, nor does anyone else, and with regard to my explorations here I do not find this overly concerning. I am not concerned with such speculative reflection because I am focused on and working to unfold with precision and accuracy the character and implications of far more concrete, immediate, and diverse aspects of reality.

I am taking care here to make clear that one pressing, concrete and immediate aspect of our moral lives is the horror of "yes-violated," that is, the horror of evil. There must be nothing escapist or naive about our realization that gracious love is ultimate, for there is no escape from the brokenness of our world. We ever have and short of some utterly unprecedented, literal, *ad extra* intervention, we ever will live in this vale of tears. So we must resolutely refuse to close our eyes to evil. We must not transvalue our values. We must not say "yes" to the brokenness of the world. We must not move beyond good and evil by means of any denial of the reality of evil. We must not pretend that there is some miraculous pill that can cut short the sorrow, grief and/or anger we experience in the face of evil.[6] There is indeed a time for tears.

To reiterate, we should in no way deny horrible aspects of reality. I can imagine traumas so intimate and horrible they are overwhelming. We are all vulnerable. However, while I want to remain exquisitely sensitive to evil as an intractable and potent reality, I also acknowledge a distinction between the focused, potentially debilitating experience of "no" in those moments when our attention is seized wholly by horror and, on the other hand, our considered understanding of the decisive asymmetry and of its significance for primordial and ultimate affirmation and joy, even as our eyes remain wide open to evil.

IN SUM: THE DECISIVE ASYMMETRY AND "YES" AS PRIMORDIAL AND ULTIMATE

Just as we know moments when we are wholly taken up in transcending joy or delight, we know moments when we are wholly overcome by horror. Indeed, transcending moments of bliss are almost always fleeting precisely because we live in this vale of tears and do not look away from the hurtful realities that so quickly intrude into moments of pure joy and recapture our attention. Nonetheless, while we affirm both of these incommensurable aspects of moral reality—good and evil (i.e., "yes-violated")—as equally real to life, we realize not only that good and evil are not simultaneous but also that they are not equiprimordial. That is, we recognize the decisive asymmetry.

In sum, we say an absolute and enduring "no" to aspects of this world, but only because we are seized in and by a more primordial and ultimate love, and so our ultimate fidelity and hope lies in a "yes" to reality that sets us against evil. Seized by the "yes" that stands behind and empowers every "no," we are moved to celebrate and support good and to decry and resist evil. Our anguish is fired by a more primordial "yes." Evil is derivative, for any evil is at root

---

6. I am not here reflecting on (and I am no expert in) grief counseling, but perhaps all this can help us to recognize a powerful spiritual resource when we are overcome by the brokenness of the world: Faces and the Face to Face. As I will detail below, it is not a matter of denying or looking away from the horror but of *also* looking and finding spiritual nourishment in the faces/Faces that still surround us. For those of us who have been profoundly and intimately wounded, the first Face may need to be simply and utterly without guile, a garden plant or a tree sprig that takes tending, or perhaps a kitten or a puppy. In the same way, some of us, in the wake of profound loss, know what it is to find spiritual nourishment in the Faces and in the transcending joy of mutual, Face-to-Face communion with our children or grandchildren, or what it is to find spiritual solace in a garden, a forest glen, or beside a quiet stream.

a "yes-violated." Good, first moral and then aesthetic, is real and substantive. Agape, the love of the having been seized, is the primordial and ultimate reality.

The critical, wonderful recognition, then, flows from precise realization of the dynamics of our pain and sorrow, from recognition that "no!" turns on a foundational and unshakable sense of what *should be*, from a sense for wellbeing awfully violated. We realize that a "yes" fires the passion in every "no." And here is the wholly reasonable and wondrous result: eyes wide open to all the evil, pain, suffering, and injustice, we nonetheless are *not* led to testify to life qualified ultimately by despair and self-condemnation, we are *not* led to the conclusion concerning life that Nietzsche attributed to the wisest in every age—ultimately, "life: *it's no good*"—for we are awakened to the fact that life is qualified first and last by love.[7]

The passion of our "yes," far from being compromised, rejected, or contradicted by "no," is powerfully and irresistibly manifest precisely when it is standing behind and inspiring a passionate "no." Every "no" is the expression of a "yes-violated," and so the realization that love is primordial and ultimate, alpha and omega, the realization that love is God, that God is love, is manifest powerfully and profoundly not only in moments of pure moral or aesthetic joy but also precisely when we stare in horror, eyes wide open to the evils suffusing this world.

Because we are seized in and by love for all the Faces that surround us, we never look away from the pain, suffering, and injustice suffusing this world. But we live nonetheless in the light of a love that is pure, primordial, and ultimate (i.e., eternal). We live in the light of the ultimacy of an enduring "yes," in the light of the affirmation behind and energizing every "no," in the light of an affirmation of all that is moral and delightful, and, as I will make explicit in the next chapter, in the light of an eyes-wide-open affirmation of others and also of ourselves as primordially and ultimately beloved.

Evil most certainly can disrupt the transcending joy (though not the profound, enduring, sustaining meaningfulness) of the Face to Face, but evil does not disrupt primordial having been seized in and by love for Faces (though, again, we all are vulnerable to horrors so extreme and intimate that we may be psychologically and/or physically debilitated). We can now realize how, without denying or closing our eyes to the reality of evil, and without sacrificing our intellectual integrity, we can celebrate and live into having been seized in and by a love that is primordial and ultimate. All of this explains how, in response to the first fold of the threefold challenge of affirmation—namely, "can we say a primordial and ultimate "yes" to reality?"—we can offer a wholehearted and sure, if precisely qualified, "yes."

To be sure, we do not say "yes" to the reality of pain, suffering, and injustice. We do not escape this vale of tears. We do wholly reasonably realize, however,

---

7. Friedrich Nietzsche, *The Anti-Christ, Ecce Homo, Twilight of the Idols, and Other Writings*, trans. A. Judith Norman, ed. Aaron Ridley (Cambridge: Cambridge University Press, 2005), 162.

that while evil is real, the very recognition of evil *as such* unveils the truth that, concerning reality, love is primordial and ultimate, alpha and omega. The dynamics of having been seized in and by love for all Faces allow us—without denial and utterly reasonably—to accept, celebrate, and proclaim that the primordial and ultimate reality is the "yes" of agape. So, again, in response to the first fold of the threefold challenge of affirmation—"can we say a primordial and ultimate 'yes' to reality?"—we can say a wholehearted and sure, if precisely qualified, "yes."

Chapter 6

Concerning Others
and Ourselves

Primordially and Ultimately, "Yes"

When our eyes are opened wide to all the pain, suffering, and injustice suffusing reality we are confronted with a threefold spiritual challenge: first, the challenge of saying a primordial and ultimate "yes" to reality; and second and third, the challenge of hearing a primordial and ultimate "yes" to others and to ourselves. I have explained how we can be empowered to say a primordial and ultimate, if precisely qualified, "yes" to reality. I will now explain how we can respond to the second and third challenges: given that we are inextricably bound up with this world, that is, that we are inextricably complicit, and are, moreover, ourselves culpable of evil, can we honestly hear a primordial and ultimate "yes" to others and to ourselves?

NO DENIAL

Let us acknowledge from the start that just like the primordial and ultimate "yes" to reality, the primordial and ultimate "yes" to others and to ourselves will be precisely qualified. For just as "yes" to primordial and ultimate reality would lack integrity and resilience if it were derived only from good and joyful occasions or involved denial or looking away from the suffering and evil suffusing reality, so "yes" to others and ourselves would lack integrity and resilience if it were realized in denial of the fact that we are inextricably bound up with and so are complicit with all the evil, or in denial of the fact that we are ourselves culpable of willful evil, of inattention and neglect, of causing harm. So we should frankly admit our complicity in this vale of tears. We should also frankly acknowledge that our choices, intentions, desires, and actions are often not good and loving, but selfish, neglectful, and even harmful to others. In sum, you and I, all of us, are complicit and personally culpable.

There should be no tolerance for naive idealism, no tolerance for denying the truth in understanding the world in part in terms of a *Realpolitik*, no tolerance for failure to acknowledge the (pardon the horrible expression) "dog eat dog" way the "real world really works," no tolerance for failure to recognize the greed, viciousness, and pure spitefulness that characterize the lives and actions of so many people.

We should be careful to name and attend to the moral dimension of reality, to the dimension of reality revealed in our having been seized in and by love for all the Faces that surround us. Of course, we acknowledge that moments when we are wholly seized in and by love for the Faces of others are exceptional. Typically, we oscillate on a continuum between living primarily out of concern for our own interests and desires and living by faith (i.e., living surrender to having been seized in and by love for all Faces). Happily, there is every reason to expect that as we work to heighten our awakening to the Faces of all others, we will live ever more fully into having been seized in and by love. Insofar as we live within this vale of tears, however, most all of us will continually oscillate between more and less fidelity to agape. And again, we always acknowledge and deal realistically with the "real" world.

None of this undercuts realization that love is primordial and ultimate, and so we can still say a primordial and ultimate "yes" to reality. Furthermore, for reasons I will now detail, none of this undercuts a primordial and ultimate "yes" to others and to ourselves. To be sure, our enduring complicity and culpability will require a precise qualification of this "yes." There will always be a certain duality to our spiritual understanding of others and of ourselves. Nonetheless, we will see that without any denial and, to the contrary, precisely with explicit, utterly unvarnished naming of our enduring complicity and culpability, the primordial and ultimate word each of us can and should hear to and for ourselves is "yes."

MAKING IT EXPLICIT: "YES" TO OURSELVES

The most reasonable and full account of reality will include not only recognition of what predominant modern Western rationality defines as "physical" reality but also recognition of moral reality, recognition of the reality of agape, recognition of "yes-violated" (i.e., of evil) and of ethical good.[1] Awakening to this reality

---

1. I explain and defend this affirmation of the reality of agape in detail in *A Reasonable Belief: Why God and Faith Make Sense* (Louisville, KY: Westminster John Knox Press, 2015).

brings home realization that, however conflicted and imperfect we each may be, we are primordially and ultimately response-able beings who have been seized in and by love for all Faces.

Significantly, in and with this spiritual realization the most critical work with regard to accepting "yes" to ourselves has already been completed, for the "yes" to ourselves is already contained within the reality of having been seized in and by love for the Faces of others. For when we are seized in and by love for the Faces of others we are ourselves—out of view of our direct notice and concern, which is first focused on the Faces of others—*we are ourselves seized in and by that same love, a love that is primordial and ultimate.*

That is, despite the fact that we are inextricably bound up in all the suffering and injustice of this world, despite the complicity that is in history always already ours, and despite our intentional failings (no matter how horrible), we ourselves have nonetheless always already been taken up in and by love, because the very love in and by which we have been seized when we find ourselves seized in and by love for the Faces of others is also, indirectly but decisively, a love that has always already seized and said a primordial and ultimate "yes" to us.

Having been seized in and by love is always primarily and directly a having been seized in and by love for the Faces of others. But while our attention in the dynamic of realized response-ability is first focused on the Faces of others, *in the having been seized we ourselves are seized in and by love. That is, we ourselves are indirectly but decisively taken up in and by love, the very same love in and by which we are seized for the Faces of others. Insofar as this love is primordial and ultimate, and insofar as we are awakened to having been seized in and by love, we find and know ourselves primordially and ultimately as beloved.*

Before attempting to unfold the dynamics of this reality more precisely, let me pause and reiterate that, as was the case with our "yes" to primordial and ultimate reality, I will not be inferring or establishing the spiritual truth of this "yes" to ourselves through argument in the modern, foundationalist (let alone empiricist) sense. I will not attempt through rigorous reflection to *conclude* that we can validly infer "yes" to ourselves, as if I am at base stepping back conceptually, reasoning, and then dispassionately drawing a conclusion about some spiritual reality (the idea of making such epistemological moves in every area of inquiry was a central fantasy of mainstream modern Western philosophy). It is rather, as will become evident, that rigorous reflection helps awaken us to this reality, rigorous reflection helps us to understand, to realize consciously and so more fully to inhabit, embrace, and celebrate the paradise of "yes" that has always already indirectly but decisively seized each one of us—if only we awaken to it.

SELF-FORGETFUL, NOT SELF-NEGATING

In the dynamic of having been seized in and by love for the Faces of others we are self-forgetful. However, and this is the crux of the matter with regard to elucidating overtly the "yes" to ourselves that attends our having been seized in and by love for the Faces of others, *this self-forgetfulness is not self-negating.* To the contrary, on reflection people remember precisely such glorious moments—the moments when we have been wholly seized in and by love for the gazelle, the flea or, when the dynamic is not moral but aesthetic, when we are wholly taken up in the beauty of a sunset, a brilliant rainbow, mountain vistas, or the *aurora borealis*—we remember precisely such glorious moments as the most rich, full, intense, and meaningful moments of our lives, the moments when we feel most real, most affirming and affirmed, most significant, most convicted over the reality and significance of good (or its violation) and beauty, most vibrantly alive. Not only are such moments of self-forgetfulness not self-negating, they are the most meaning-full and fulfilling moments of our lives.

Notably, the glory of having been seized in and by love for the Faces of others may, depending on context, stimulate either joy ("yes" to "yes") or horror ("no" to "yes-violated"). The decisive asymmetry affirms "yes" as ultimate and constant. Again, "no" is a derivative moment dependent on the having been seized, for the "no" expresses a reaction to "yes-violated," which is how "yes" is manifest in contexts of injustice or suffering. That is, the fullness of meaning and the gift of the "yes" of living having been seized in and by love is realized whether one is reacting to what is delightful or wonderful (where one happily shares in joy, where one may even share in the transcending joy of mutually awakened, Face-to-Face communion) or whether one is reacting to what is harmful or unjust (where one is horrified, full of conviction, and, if possible, rushing to resist or give aid). Unless, as we have already discussed, we suffer from physical or psychological debilitation because of the extremity and intimacy of the violation, in such moments we find ourselves taken up in the meaning-rich "yes" of having been seized in and by love for the Faces of others.

In sum, the most meaning-full, vibrant, and significant moments of our lives are the most radically self-forgetful. While self-forgetful, however, they are not self-negating, precisely because they are indeed the most meaning-full, vibrant, and significant moments of our lives. The enemy of spiritual meaning and of "yes," then, is not evil ("yes-violated") but insensitivity to the Faces of others, a hardened heart. I will now attempt to unfold more precisely the dynamics of "yes" to ourselves, a "yes" that is always already given in having been seized in and by love.

A PERILOUS PARADOX: TO THE DEGREE I FOCUS ON ESTABLISHING MYSELF, I LOSE MYSELF

At this juncture we would do well to note a perilous paradox in the dynamics of affirmation in and through agape: Namely, I cut myself off from "yes" insofar as I am focused on self-assertion and self-justification, on grounding and establishing myself, on *my own* "yes" to myself. For insofar as I am focused on establishing myself, I obstruct my own awakening to the "yes" of the having been seized in and by love for the Faces of others and remain fatally tied to a struggle to win through to wholly autonomous self-affirmation.

The path to "yes," by contrast, depends on allowing oneself to be awakened all the more fully to having been seized in and by love for others. For only insofar as I surrender to having been seized in and by love for other Faces am I awakened to my own indirect but decisive having been seized in and by love. The sad irony of the devastating dynamic of wholly autonomous struggles to affirm oneself, then, is that the more one focuses on oneself and one's own needs and desires, the more one tries directly to affirm and establish oneself, the more one is thereby isolated and cut off from the "yes" of having been seized in and by love.

By this point the magnitude and stakes of the error involved in the modern Western presumption that the atomistic "I" is at the core of personal identity and thinking is clear. By beginning from the atomistic self, modern Western thought conceptually inhibits our ability to *receive* ourselves from the first. To speak technically for a moment, the radically atomistic and solipsistic epistemology and ontology of Descartes's "I think, therefore I am," which took the atomistic "I" as an Archimedean point, was disastrous even before it was subject to the empiricist reduction that delivered us unto full-blown scientism. In the wake of the scientistic reduction long predominant in modern Western rationality, the realm of spirit, of free will, of moral reality, of what Descartes delineated as an independent realm of mind/spirit in contrast to the realm of things, has been decimated.

Insofar as an analogue to the classic idea of a "mind," "spirit," or "self" has been preserved in mainstream modern Western thought, it has been preserved under the aegis of "intention," that is, under the aegis of the capacity of humans and perhaps a few other mammals (and, in theory, qualifying extraterrestrials) to adopt a conceptual and imaginative stance over and against the rest of the world and to form intentions (or, to speak more exactly, since scientism makes no concession to free will here, the capacity of humans to have intentions formed in their brains). This capacity for intentionality, which emerges out of the basic stuff of existence in sufficiently complex beings, is taken by predominant streams of modern Western rationality to be ultimate and primordial insofar as any creature is "spiritual," has "mind" or "soul," and/or qualifies ethically as a "person."[2]

From the modern scientistic perspective, then, we are primordially and ultimately atomistic "I's" with the capacity to distinguish ourselves out from the rest of existence insofar as we possess a conceptual capacity to set ourselves up (or, again, in accord with rigorous scientism, to have formed in our brain an idea of ourselves as set up) over and against all others and all else. Of course, this struggle to distinguish and establish oneself does not happen in a vacuum. One strives to establish oneself over and against concrete others. In this sense, the defined character of the modern Western intentional self is identical to the

---

2. To be clear, in opposition to materialism/physicalism I am offering a qualified affirmation of Descartes's delineation of a sphere of spirit. At the same time, I am criticizing Descartes's unqualified, atomistic individualism, which in recent thought endures in terms of "intentionality."

lived character of the self that is captured by desire for personal survival and realization of maximum power vis-à-vis all others, for modernity's intentional "I" is first and last atomistic and oppositional. Henceforth I will refer to these dynamics as the "logic of domination."[3]

To be sure, the modern "I" may pursue its enlightened self-interest. At points the modern "I" may cooperate instead of compete (there may be both selfish and cooperative genes and memes). But such Hobbesian pursuit still leaves it locked within the self-interested dynamics of the logic of domination (or, in some evolutionary variants, leaves the I duped by its genes into sacrificing its individual interests for the sake of the gene pool or kinship group). Groups of modern "I's" joined by common, enlightened self-interest may even form effective collectives and develop Hobbesian or Darwinian styled "ethics," but the devastating logic of domination conceptually cuts them off from the spiritual ties that bind true communities of Faces.

Predominant modern Western rationality's locked-in, atomistic existential stance (e.g., the intentional stance) cuts off any openness to having been seized in and by love—because having been seized in and by love is not the product of any human decision or intention. Within the confines of this confused and truncated rationality, self-originating assertion is the only thinkable starting point (to the degree we are thought to possess true agentival capacities at all), and some sort of Hobbesian attempt to "enlighten" and so make a pseudo-virtue out of selfishness (i.e., enlightened self-interest, which is still essentially selfish) is the only way toward any simulacra of real morality and morally grounded ethics. In sum, tragically, what follows from the predominant, fundamentally atomistic, modern Western understanding of selfhood is devastating self-enclosure, spiritual nihilism, and the bottomless power plays of the logic of domination.

Let me pause to reaffirm that surely the modern scientific account of the "physical" origins of our universe, planet, and of our biological evolution and emergence as incredibly complex organisms is basically accurate. But the vocabulary and rationality of modern science is too narrow to tell the whole story. For in relation to reality that lies outside the materialist methodological boundaries (and hence beyond the possible detection) of modern science, I know myself fundamentally and originally as a spiritual being in my response-ability, in having been seized in and by love for the Faces of others. As I argue in detail in *A Reasonable Belief: Why God and Faith Make Sense*, it is critical to distinguish the illegitimate and hegemonic pretensions of scientism from legitimate science (which should be affirmed and celebrated). Concomitant to that philosophical task is the spiritual task that I am presently focused on: namely, the task of reawakening ourselves to the reality that both physically/biologically (always

3. I develop the category of the "logic of domination" in contrast to the "logic of dominion" at length in chapter 7, "Dominion versus Domination: Living Life and Living Death," in William Greenway, *For the Love of All Creatures: The Story of Grace in Genesis* (Grand Rapids: William B. Eerdmans Publishing Co., 2015), 106–24.

obvious from an evolutionary perspective) and also spiritually, we are first of all not isolated, atomistic selves.

Contrary to predominant and spiritually devastating modern conceptual trajectories, there is no originary assertion, decision, or intention in or by humans (or dolphins, qualifying extra-terrestrials, and so forth) that primordially and ultimately distinguishes and grounds our being. Insofar as our spiritual being is first manifest in our response-ability, we do not first and truly exist prior to and over and against others but, to the contrary, we exist precisely *through* having been seized in and by love for all Faces. In this sense the spiritual reality of our be-ing is delivered through others—including not only the dolphins and (in principle) qualifying extra-terrestrials but also through the lions, wolves, fleas, and saplings (the more the richer!)—for we first and truly receive ourselves as primordially and ultimately response-able, beloved beings in and through our having been seized in and by love for the Faces of others.

The "yes" to our selves is indirect, because it is realized in the event of having been seized in and by love for the Faces of others—we are the latter Face in every Face to Face—but it is nonetheless decisive. Insofar as we are morally awakened to the glory of having been seized in and by love for the Faces of others, we find ourselves already established, welcomed, accepted, and beloved, members of a spiritual communion. In reality, then, we are not primordially and first, let alone ultimately, discrete "I's," isolated centers of emergent consciousness, for from the first we emerge as spiritual beings in and from a community formed and sustained by love.

FORGIVENESS: WITHOUT DENIAL, "YES" TO OTHERS

There is a place for assessment of the faces of Faces. Assessment of faces is critical, for instance, when we make judgments about someone's character, wisdom, intelligence, or knowledge and their potential for being our doctor, pastor, friend, spouse, or "animal" companion. Nonetheless, having been seized in and by love for the Faces of others is not dependent on how desirable or undesirable others are to and for us, or on their intelligence, professional competence, or any other like consideration. Insofar as we are morally awake we find ourselves seized in and by love for the Faces of others regardless of the character of their faces, whether they be lion, gazelle, flea, or human, whether they be friend or enemy, good or evil, awake or self-incurved.

Most important for our reflection at this juncture is the realization that having been seized in and by love for Faces is not dependent on the degree to which others are good or evil. Christians (like me) traditionally highlight the supra-ethical character of the having been seized by deliberately speaking of "grace" in contrast to "love," by specifying that grace is amazing because it is love that is not deserved, love that embraces us despite our complicity and culpability. That is a fine and helpful linguistic distinction, but by this point it is clear that what Christians refer to as grace is already contained in the love for Faces in and by which we find ourselves seized, for this love names a having been seized that comes not only from outside of ourselves, but from outside of history, and so it means love that abides apart from any consideration (including any ethical consideration) within the realm of faces. In other words, grace is intrinsic to having been seized in and by love for Faces (to say "gracious love," then, is a redundancy stressing that agape is primordial and ultimate).

As the reference to Christian grace suggests, the reality of having been seized in and by love for all Faces without regard to evil is commonly discussed using the everyday language of "forgiveness."[4] Our discussion helps to make clear just what is "given" in forgiveness and just how radically "fore" is the "given-ness." What is "given" is, speaking precisely, the gift of love, for forgiveness is the gift of having been seized in and by love for the Faces of others. This love for others is always already "fore" because it is primordially and ultimately something we receive, something we receive in having been seized in and by love for all Faces. For insofar as our having been seized in and by love for all Faces is a having been seized before/outside of history and ethics, we find ourselves always already having forgiven all Faces.

Forgiving, then, is not a product of our own decision or initiative. It is not something that we give, let alone something we decide to give. For insofar as we are awakened to having been seized in and by love for the Faces of others who are inescapably complicit and who are inevitably more or less evil, who may even be unjust toward us personally, we find that we have already forgiven them. That is, we are primordially and ultimately in a state of forgiveness in relation to them, for we have been seized in and by love for their Faces (if not for their faces). In this sense, insofar as we are fully awake and living in the light of having been seized in and by love for all Faces—and admittedly, in this vale of tears we typically live in occluded light at best—but insofar as we do live in the light of having been seized in and by love for all Faces, we love even enemies of the moral, even as they remain enemies.

"HAVING FORGIVEN," NOT "FORGETTING"

It is critical not to confuse "having forgiven" with "forgetting." *Forgiveness* vis-à-vis *Faces* does not imply *forgetfulness* vis-à-vis *faces*. To forgive is to be seized in and by love for the Faces despite the complicity and culpability of the faces. But to forget would be to ignore, to fail to notice or to deny faces' complicity and culpability. To forget, then, would be unrealistic, would amount to losing touch with the

---

4. My discussion of forgiveness here is a lightly edited adaptation of my discussion of forgiveness in chapter 8, "Justice, Grace, Forgiveness" of *A Reasonable Belief*. My position remains essentially unchanged. *A Reasonable Belief* provides a far more in-depth and complete defense of the philosophical spirituality informing this work, which focuses wholly and with far more depth on the challenge of evil.

ongoing realities of life within this vale of tears, would signal a failure to recognize the critical place for assessment of faces, and would involve denial of real evil.

We love the Face but not the face of the one who is acting as enemy of the moral. While we love all Faces, then, not only do we not forget faces, but for the sake of the moral, for the sake of love, for the sake of wronged Faces, we take decisive (in extreme instances violent or even lethal) action over and against faces that perpetuate evil and injustice. Never, of course, do we take decisive or violent action out of hatred or vengefulness, but only insofar as we must in order to protect vulnerable Faces.

Emmanuel Levinas, who informs so much of my reflection here, was, as discussed, a Jewish labor-camp survivor who wrote in the wake of the Nazi horror. When Levinas speaks of being taken hostage by the Face of the other in a realm outside of history, he has in mind the Faces not only of friends and allies, but the Faces of his Nazi captors, the Faces even of the Nazis who murdered his family. When Levinas speaks about our infinite love for *every* Face, he even has the Faces of those Nazis in mind.

But for Levinas, to be seized by the Face is not to forget the face. Levinas maintained that when the face of the Face by which one is seized is unjust and evil then, for the sake of wronged Faces, one resists the actions of that "yes-violating" face.[5] Accordingly, Levinas was not a pacifist. He was an officer in the French armed forces. Nonetheless, when Levinas testifies to the way the Face seizes us from beyond any particulars of the face, from beyond history, he is testifying to the way in which the Faces even of captors and murderers seize us, he is testifying to a love in and by which we are seized for the Faces even of enemies of the moral, even as their faces remain enemy, perhaps even as they kill us, or even as we resist or fight them, perhaps even as we kill them in defense of the Faces they are killing. In any case, forgiveness vis-à-vis Faces does not imply forgetfulness vis-à-vis faces.

The having forgiven intrinsic to having been seized in and by love for others makes clear how we are able to say a primordial and ultimate "yes" to others. In sum, it is now evident how, eyes wide open to evil, we are seized by and can say a primordial and ultimate "yes" to reality, and how, eyes wide open to evil, we are seized by and can say a primordial and ultimate "yes" to others. Let me now clarify how we are seized by and can say a primordial and ultimate "yes" to ourselves.

FORGIVEN-NESS: WITHOUT DENIAL, "YES" TO OURSELVES

Clarity about the way in which we are seized in and by love for the Faces of others despite their complicity and culpability is critical to full articulation of the dynamics of the "yes" to each of us. For what is revealed in our having been seized in and by love for all those other Faces despite the complicity and

5. For those familiar with Levinas, let me note that I am here referencing what he discusses in terms of "the third."

culpability of their faces, no matter how awful, is the character of the love by which we have been seized. Namely, what is revealed is an indirect but decisive love for one's own Face which is wholly given despite one's own complicity and culpability, no matter how awful.

Insofar as my awakening to having been seized in and by love for all Faces is indirectly but decisively a "yes" to my own Face, and insofar as having been seized in and by love for others' Faces is given despite the complicity and culpability of their faces, no matter how awful, that same "yes" is given to me despite my own complicity and culpability, no matter how awful. Awakened to the gift of having been seized in and by love, I find myself not only having forgiven others, but also living my own having been forgiven-ness. I find myself living—without evasion or denial, eyes wide open to my own complicity and culpability—the realization that the primordial and ultimate word to every Face, including my own, is "yes." I too am primordially and ultimately loved, primordially and ultimately beloved.

In having forgiven and having been forgiven, then, what has been given both to us and to others is love, the love in and by which we have always already been seized. We find ourselves having forgiven and having been forgiven not only beyond any justification or expectation but contrary to every justification and expectation. This is miraculous, amazing love because we find ourselves justified without justification, expiated without expiation, complicit and culpable and yet seized wholly and fully in and by love for all Faces, including our own.

Awakened to having been seized in and by love for all Faces, we live and move in the light of the glorious reality of incomprehensible, gracious love, in the "yes" of an amazing grace. I am not arguing for or explaining this love. Rather, I am striving to awaken readers to having been seized in and by this love so that all may know its reality, be keen to live in its glorious light, and be eager to testify to it in hopes of awakening others to the joy of living surrender to the having been seized. All of this eyes wide open to the horrors of this vale of tears, to others' complicity and culpability, and to our own complicity and culpability, but living having forgiven others and having been forgiven.

Let me digress momentarily and take care to say that recognition of yourself as beloved means that if someone tries to violate your Face, you should be just as responsible to your own beloved Face as you would be to any other Face. Thus you should take decisive and perhaps, insofar as it is necessary, violent action in defense of your own Face. There is nothing good, loving, or faithful about allowing yourself to be taken advantage of or abused. The love that moves you to affirm and defend other Faces should equally move you to affirm and defend your own beloved Face if you are being treated unjustly.[6]

6. My neo-Levinasian affirmation of self-defense flows from a spiritual stance that differs from modern affirmations of self-defense based on appeal to self-assertion or assertion of the intrinsic value of the atomistic "I." For my call to defense and affirmation of self flows from the "yes" of having been seized in and by love for all Faces, and this includes, indirectly but decisively, having been seized in and by love for my own Face.

FORGIVENESS/FORGIVEN-NESS AND
SELF-INCURVED (ANESTHETIZED, UNAWAKE) FACES

Your own having been forgiven-ness is not in any way dependent on the moral awakening of others. In particular, your having been forgiven-ness is not dependent on having been forgiven by anyone else. For, again, our own forgiven-ness does not flow from others but from the gracious character of the having been seized. Others do not themselves give forgiveness to us but, insofar as they have been seized in and by love for the Faces of others, enter themselves into a state of having forgiven us and, indirectly but decisively, into a state of having been forgiven themselves. Our having been forgiven is not dependent on the awakening of any other, then, for the forgiveness is given not by any other but in our having been seized in and by love.

While our having been forgiven is not dependent on the awakening of any other, there are significant stakes in others' awakenings. For their awakening signals their living in the light of the having been seized in and by love for your Face, just as you live in the light of having been seized in and by love for their Faces. With mutual awakening to having been seized in and by love for one another's Faces, one's joy in and with others can be made complete, for then there arises the possibility that we might live not only having forgiven/ having been forgiven, then there arises the possibility that we might participate in the transcending joy of mutually awakened and mutually seized Face to Face communion.

To review, the affirmation we receive for our own Faces flows from a spiritual stance that is precisely opposite from those paradigmatically modern understandings of self-defense and self-sacrifice that turn on appeal to unrestricted autonomy, self-assertion, or assertion of the intrinsic value of the atomistic "I" and its right to be (an assertion that in modern thought stands without any background justification, that is, it is sheer assertion). Our call to affirmation of our own Faces flows from the "yes" of having been seized in and by love for all Faces, including, indirectly but decisively, having been seized in and by love for our own Faces. All of this unveils the non-atomistic, non-self-originating, radically communal character of our primordial be-ing as Faces: we are each of us really and ultimately the gifts of primordial and ultimate love.

ON THE SYMMETRY BETWEEN HAVING
FORGIVEN AND HAVING BEEN FORGIVEN

"To forgive" is not something that we initiate or do. Forgiveness of others is originally given to us in the love in and by which we are seized. That is, forgiveness of others is something we receive insofar as we live surrender to having been seized in and by love for the Faces of others despite the complicity and culpability of their faces. Having been ourselves forgiven is simultaneously given to us by that same love. Indeed, having forgiven others and having been forgiven ourselves both name the work of the same having been seized in and by love, but in relation to others' Faces on the one hand and in relation to our own Faces on the other. Thus there is always a perfect symmetry between having forgiven and having been forgiven. We live having been forgiven ourselves precisely insofar as we live having forgiven others—not because there is any causal relationship between having forgiven and having been forgiven, but because both are realized as living realities for us in the same measure: namely, insofar as we surrender to having been seized in and by love. To the degree that we are awake to having been seized in and by love for all Faces, we live the reality of having forgiven and having been forgiven.[7]

Sadly, those not awake to having been seized in and by love for all Faces remain ensnared within the logic of domination (i.e., the quest to establish oneself over and against all others) and, despite perhaps desperate attempts to deny or ignore it, remain under the weight of their complicity and culpability. Those who live surrender to having been seized in and by love for all Faces (i.e., those who live faith in God) are freed to the "yes" of having forgiven and having been forgiven even as they frankly confess their own complicity and culpability. They are freed to live in the light of love and affirmation, to live in the light of having forgiven and having been forgiven, for they are freed to live in the light of "yes" to every Face, including an eyes wide open "yes" to their own Faces.

HAVING BEEN FORGIVEN-NESS AND THE ACKNOWLEDGMENT OF COMPLICITY AND CULPABILITY

Because living in the light of having been seized in and by love for every Face involves no forgetfulness about faces, no shutting of one's eyes to the pain, suffering, and injustices suffusing reality, and no denial of complicity and culpability, life lived in the light of the primordial and ultimate "yes," that is, life lived in surrender to having been seized in and by love for all Faces, the life of faith, is immediately, continually, and inherently life lived in the realm of having forgiven and having been forgiven. What is amazing is our realization that in our having been seized in and by love for every Face, unmitigated affirmation of ourselves despite even our own complicity and culpability (i.e., having been forgiven-ness) is always already accomplished. It is accomplished before and beyond any explanatory ethical logic within history, without any effort or initiative on our part (save we do not harden our hearts), and apart

---

7. This is how we can understand Jesus when he says that we only receive forgiveness ourselves insofar as we forgive others. It is not that there is some tit-for-tat relationship between our forgiveness of others and God's forgiveness of us, as if our forgiveness of others is a precondition of God's forgiving of us, but because through the gift of grace we simultaneously, in the same dynamic, receive (or harden our hearts to) forgiveness of others and for ourselves.

from any of those (often bloody) would-be expiatory mechanisms that traffic in tit-for-tat economies.

Insofar as you live in the light of having been seized in and by love for every Face, you live having been seized in and by love eyes wide open in this vale of tears, you live having been seized in and by love even for enemies of the moral, you live the freedom and affirmation of having forgiven and having been forgiven, and in relation to those who also live in the light and so see our Faces, you live the transcending joy of mutual, Face-to-Face communion. Again, we do not reason our way to, conclude, or infer this reality. It is the gift of the having been seized. Awakened to the reality, we confess it, enjoy it, give thanks for it, testify to it, and strive to live ever more fully in its light.

Realization of having been forgiven-ness brings with it a desire to forgive others all the more fully, and to acknowledge ever more fully your own complicity and culpability. The desire to confess ever more fully is not the manifestation of a sadistic drive to diminish or attack yourself. To the contrary, the desire to confess ever more fully is stimulated in the realization that with more complete confession comes ever more complete release, freedom, and joy. For insofar as your complicity and culpability is exposed to the light of the love of the having been seized, condemnation is burned away. On the other hand, to the degree you hide your complicity or culpability in a fog of denial, deflections, and/or rationalizations but remain alive to your response-ability (i.e., remain awakened to other Faces), you burn with self-condemnation. Thus you have the desire to confess ever more fully in order to expose the associated condemnation to the expiating light of the having been seized.

In short, in the light of the love of the having been seized you find yourself always already having forgiven and always already having been forgiven. Realization of having been forgiven-ness sets in motion an ordered, spiraling dynamic between release from the weight of complicity and culpability on the one hand, and ever more complete acknowledgement of complicity and culpability (i.e., confession) on the other. Namely, the joyous release of the having been seized stimulates the confidence and desire to confess all the more fully, which makes the joyous release ever more complete. In short, it is not guilt that stimulates confession but the release from guilt that flows from awakening that stimulates confession, which brings fuller release, which increases the impetus to confession, which brings fuller release, and so on.

To those who remain captive to the logic of domination, the vulnerability of this utter abandonment of self-assertion and self-justification can appear to be hopelessly weak, even existentially suicidal. But in reality, to the degree you seek to justify yourself, or protest your innocence by minimizing or denying culpability and complicity, you confusedly harm yourself by shielding real culpability and complicity from the light, and thus, to the degree you still remain alive to Faces and to your own Face, that is, to the degree the reality of agape remains a force against which you must harden your heart, you remain bound to the burning weight of complicity and culpability. On the other hand, far from

being existentially vulnerable or suicidal, utter abandonment of self-assertion
and self-justification, that is, wholesale surrender *to* having been seized in and
by love for all Faces, including your own, leaves you, spiritually, unfathomably
strong, for unmitigated, eyes wide open acknowledgement of culpability and
complicity in the light of the love of the having been seized does not bring
condemnation but the fullest possible release into a paradise of "yes."[8]

In sum, insofar as we are awakened and live surrender to the gift of agape,
that is, live surrender to having been seized in and by love, live having forgiven
and having been forgiven, we are gifted with an eyes wide open, primordial and
ultimate "yes" to reality, to others, and to ourselves, we are gifted by amazing
grace. This "yes" is not unmitigated, for we do indeed keep our eyes wide open to
our enduring existence within this vale of tears, to our enduring complicity and
culpability, to all the pain, suffering, and injustice. The conclusion Nietzsche
attributes to the "wisest men in every age" concerning life, "*it's no good*," does
have a delimited place.[9] But Nietzsche fails to discern the decisive asymmetry,
and so he fails to appreciate the dynamics of having been seized in and by love,
he remains conceptually shut off from amazing grace, and he is driven to a
desperate, spiritually devastating, anti-moral recommendation.

We keep our eyes wide open to enduring evil, and we confess complicity and
culpability, but we are not overcome or condemned insofar as, abandoning every
assertion of a right to be, of a right to our place in the sun, we live by faith, that
is, we live surrender to having been seized in and by love, and so we live having
forgiven and having been forgiven. Insofar as we live surrender to having been
seized in and by love for all Faces we are not overcome by the three-fold spiritual
challenge of affirmation in the face of evil for, wholly reasonably and without
denial, evasion, or guilt, we live in the light of a primordial and ultimate "yes" to
reality, to others, and to ourselves, and when our delimited attention is wholly
taken up in moments of pure joy, we are free, in all innocence, to revel in joy.

8. So Jesus says in Luke 9:24: "those who want to save their life will lose it, and those who lose
their life *for my sake* [i.e., for the sake of Jesus' gospel of neighbor-love, for the sake of God, for the
sake of agape] will save it" (emphasis mine).
9. Friedrich Nietzsche, *The Anti-Christ, Ecce Homo, Twilight of the Idols, and Other Writings*,
trans. A. Judith Norman, ed. Aaron Ridley (Cambridge: Cambridge University Press, 2005), 162.

PART 3
FYODOR DOSTOEVSKY
AND JOY EYES WIDE
OPEN TO EVIL

Chapter 7

A Cautionary Tale

*Iris Murdoch on the Death
of the Atomistic "I"*

Despite the predominant modern Western stress on the absolute priority of the autonomous, atomistic, intentional "I," the notion that the death of that very "I" stands at the heart of profound spiritual enlightenment endures in modern Western culture. Indeed, the idea that the proximity of one's own death is enlightening is cliché and nonetheless true for being so common. Consider, for instance, the common trope that in the face of near-term terminal illness, when a de-centering consciousness of the death of one's "I" comes home, that it is precisely at that time when the true value of even the little things in life dawns fully (flowers smell sweeter, sunsets glow more beautifully, friendships feel more precious, loves intensify, and so forth).

One of the more profound portrayals of the revelatory power of the death of the atomistic "I" is found in noted author and philosopher Iris Murdoch's novel, *The Unicorn*.[1] However, despite the profundity of Murdoch's thought, and despite our shared alarm over Nietzschean transvaluation of morals, in the final analysis I find Murdoch's understanding to be inadequate. Notably, I will

---

1. Iris Murdoch, *The Unicorn* (London: Penguin Books, 1963). Diogenes Allen brought this example to my attention. Allen reflects on the passage cited here in *The Path of Perfect Love* (Cambridge: Cowley Publications, 1992), 11.

argue that what decisively truncates her philosophy, to which I am otherwise very close, is precisely a failure to discern the reality and significance of agape. Because of this lacuna, I will argue, even Murdoch remains ensnared by Nietzschean conceptual dynamics from which she wants to escape; and for that reason I conclude that Murdoch's account of the love that flows from the death of the atomistic I offers us a "cautionary tale."

Murdoch is an excellent conversation partner both because of her brilliance and because, I will argue, the decisive element she is missing is precisely the discernment of agape that lies at the heart of my neo-Levinasian reflection. In direct contrast to Murdoch, it is the philosophy of Dostoevsky in *The Brothers Karamazov*, oft cited by Levinas, that I will affirm in these closing chapters. I will argue that a narrative of faith that is the gift of agape, that is, a narrative of surrender to having been seized in and by love for all creatures, lies at the heart of Dostoevsky's spiritual testimony in *The Brothers Karamazov*. (This is precisely the narrative of agape that I have unfolded in a more theoretical modality in the previous two chapters.)

DE-CENTERING WITHOUT AWAKENING

I turn now to Murdoch's brilliant but ultimately abortive account of love in the wake of the death of the atomistic "I" in her novel *The Unicorn*. Effingham Cooper is a successful and vain civil servant. As the sun sets over a desolate stretch of western Ireland on the heels of a trying day, Effingham angrily rushes away from a conflict. Too absorbed in reliving the day to be careful in the barren landscape, Effingham gets hopelessly lost. After hours of increasingly frantic walking through deepening darkness he stumbles in slippery mud. Too late, he realizes he is caught in the grip of a bog. Effingham instantly realizes the threat. He has heard stories of morasses "which would engulf a man, of slimy wells and pits and sudden muddy descents into the limestone caves below."[2]

A brief, frantic struggle ends with Effingham sucked in nearly to his knees and very slowly sinking. With the sudden giving way of one foot, Effingham senses that he is on the top "brink of one of those bottomless slimy wells of the bog."[3] He is surrounded by mud. There is nothing to grab onto or push against. He is miles from the nearest road or house, and he is trapped utterly. As he continues slowly but inexorably to sink, he finds himself pitched slightly backwards. Hours later, with the first glimmering of dawn, his legs have been almost wholly consumed and the thick mud is gripping the lower part of his back. Suddenly Effingham realizes there is simply no hope of rescue. He is about to slip over the brink and with sudden rapidity, "slither down into the liquid

2. Murdoch, *Unicorn*, 165.
3. Ibid., 166.

hole that now seemed positively to be sucking at his left leg."[4] For the first time Effingham truly confronts his own death, and experiences something of the gift of the death of the atomistic "I":

> The confrontation [with death] brought with it a new quietness and a new terror. . . . Even the stars were veiled now, and Effingham was at the centre of a [dark] globe. He felt the touch of some degraded, gibbering panic . . . . He did not want to perish whimpering. As if obeying some imperative . . . he collected himself and concentrated his attention; yet what he was concentrating on was [darkness] too . . . . Why had Effingham never realized that [death] was the only fact that mattered, perhaps the only fact there was? If one had realized this, one could have lived all one's life in the light. Yet why in the light, and why did it seem now that the dark ball at which he was staring was full of light? Something had been withdrawn, had slipped away from him in the moment of his attention, and that something was simply himself . . . . Yet what was left, for something was surely left, something existed still? It came to him with the simplicity of a simple sum. What was left was everything else, all that was not himself, that object which he had never before seen and upon which he now gazed with the passion of a lover. . . . Since he was mortal he was nothing, and since he was nothing all that was not himself was filled to the brim with being, and it was from this that the light streamed. This then was love, to look and look until one exists no more, *this* was the love which was the same as death. He looked and knew, with a clarity which was one with the increasing light, that with the death of the self the world becomes quite automatically the object of a perfect love.[5]

The "death of the self" that brings "light" is not Effingham's impending death in the bog but the death of his self-centered self. Thus Effingham's poignant reflection that if only he had known this "love . . . which was the same as death" sooner, he "could have lived all [his] life in the light." Murdoch's "death" of the self-centered self that brings light, then, describes not physical death but a breaking of the self-incurvature of the logic of domination, an enlightening self-forgetfulness.

In the novel, Effingham is rescued. And with rescue, his self, his self-interested self, his "old unregenerate being," his "will to live," returns.[6] He retains some sense for the power of his "vision." He feels vaguely "transfigured." But the clarity and power of the vision fade fast. Almost immediately he is struggling to remember and explain it to others. "Before the self vanishes nothing really is," he tries to explain shortly after being rescued, "and that's how it is most of the time. But as soon as the self vanishes everything is, and becomes automatically the object of love. Love holds the world together, and if we could forget ourselves

4. Ibid.
5. Ibid., 167.
6. Ibid., 168, 172.

everything in the world would fly into perfect harmony, and when we see beautiful things that is what they remind us of."[7]

Murdoch brings home the "revelatory gift of the proximity of death" thematic with extraordinary power. Murdoch is well known for striving to rehabilitate moral language in modern philosophy and resisting Nietzsche's transvaluing of the ethical. In this passage she is attempting both to criticize modern Western individualism and simultaneously to rehabilitate something akin to the classic, agapic understanding of love in terms of selfless love. But Murdoch's vision is fatally truncated by modern Western rationality's eliding of moral reality.

Note that there is no overt moral or ethical dimension to Effingham's experience. It is no accident that Murdoch specifies that "beautiful things" remind us that, "love holds the world together." Effingham's self-forgetfulness does not take him beyond the boundaries of the aesthetic. There is no ethical or moral dimension to Effingham's experience, no having been seized in and by love for others' Faces. Indeed, Effingham's experience is stunningly devoid of any specific Faces. It is devoid not only of any of the Faces of any bog creatures (plant or animal), but devoid (stunningly, awfully devoid) of any memory of the Faces of any significant friends, lovers, enemies, or family. Indeed, specificity itself is remarkably absent from Murdoch's description. Despite the concreteness the literary form of the novel invites, Murdoch continually falls back on abstractions: "everything," "light," "world," "being," "is," "beautiful things."

Indeed, the experience remains ultimately devoid even of Effingham's own Face. Insofar as he is taken by love he is self-forgetful, his self "vanishes." Insofar as his self returns, what returns is his "old unregenerate self," the self that is an expression of his "will to power"—and through the balance of the novel the impact of this experience on Effingham and on his old, unregenerate self rapidly dissipates. The novel leaves us with an either/or between a "self that vanishes" and a self that is the expression of a "will to power." There is no return of a transformed self, no positive articulation of self-affirmation, no description of a self that is affirmed and empowered to act in a fashion that is not unregenerate. In sum, even in this passage, through which a ray of light shines in what is otherwise an unrelentingly bleak narrative, we are ultimately given only abstractions and negation and an either/or between self-creation through self-assertion ("will to power") and no self at all.

This is all the more significant because virtually all the rest of *The Unicorn* is about affirming moral reality. In the novel a "unicorn"—explicitly a Christ figure, though Murdoch's understanding is most certainly not traditional—is something of a voluntary scapegoat who guiltily suffers for wrongdoing. When the "unicorn" at the narrative center of *The Unicorn* eventually commits suicide, another character, a character who has just gotten away legally but not ethically with (literal) murder, takes her place. In short, in opposition to modernity's

---

7. Ibid., 173.

eliding of the moral, Murdoch affirms moral reality as a weighty force in human life. But nowhere does she describe any substantive, transforming, or life-affirming connection between the weight of moral reality in everyday life and the light of "perfect love" at the core of Effingham's vision.

In other words, Murdoch remains bewitched by modern Western reason's Nietzschean eliding of moral reality. Her struggle against the Nietzschean eliding of the moral is decisively compromised because her portrayal of the most radical, self-forgetful love takes place on the far side of a Nietzschean eliding of moral reality. Thus, despite her best efforts, Murdoch finds herself caught within Sartre's neo-Nietzschean either-or. For Sartre, there is either radical self-creation of my "I" through sheer free choice (what in modern thought is often called authentic existence), or there is no real "I" at all (inauthentic existence) for one is wholly a product of antecedent forces.

Unlike Sartre, Murdoch considers radical self-creation through free choice to be devoid of any real meaning. So the ultimate revelation comes with the radical self-forgetfulness of Effingham Cooper's experience. But this experience involves only a loss of self, self-forgetfulness without return. When return does come, it is the "will to power" that returns. So, again, Murdoch, caught up in neo-Nietzschean conceptual parameters, presents us finally with an either/or between self-creation through self-assertion and no self (i.e., no authentic "I") at all.

Because Murdoch develops no connection between the weight of moral forces and "perfect love," her rehabilitation of the moral delivers us to steely-eyed acknowledgment of the reality of evil without any possibility of escape. Her characters are caught forever within bloody—both figuratively and literally bloody—tit-for-tat ethical relationships and power struggles. The "unicorns" remain embroiled within the eye-for-an-eye economies of these relationships. Except for rare, fleeting moments when the self "vanishes," provisional escape from personal experience of crushing guilt comes only through varying degrees of denial and scapegoating.

The character of Murdoch's rehabilitation of the ethical is clarified when Effingham exclaims, "if we could forget ourselves everything in the world would fly into perfect harmony." This line is only believable, as Murdoch clearly intends it to be, if the only source of "disharmony" is human wrongdoing. That is, Murdoch's "harmony" *includes* natural suffering and pain (disease, injury), and it includes all the world's ugly, brute, heart-wrenching natural deaths (predation, natural disaster), for none of these would be affected by a shift to total human selflessness. In the words of Denis, who becomes the new, voluntary "unicorn" at novel's end, "Suffering is no scandal. It is natural. Nature appoints it."[8]

Murdoch's depiction of Effingham's vision in the bog can strike us as profound and true, for it is true insofar as it goes. It is in many ways a beautiful description of love and of our experience of having been seized within the boundaries of the

8. Ibid., 198.

aesthetic. But Murdoch's account of the self transformed (or, really, vanished) by love is devastatingly incomplete, for she fails to discern that ethics is rooted in agape, that is, that morality comes in our having been seized in and by love for the Faces of all creatures. As a result she does not recognize the decisive asymmetry or realize the reality of the gracious love that allows affirmation, primordially and ultimately, of reality, of all others, and of ourselves, even as we live on in this vale of tears eyes wide open to pain, suffering, and injustice, and to our own complicity and culpability.

While Murdoch succeeds to some degree in her struggle against predominant modern Western rationality's eliding of ethical reality, then, her reassertion of the reality of the ethical is short-circuited by her eliding of the reality of agape. Murdoch maintains that at the level of human relations moral forces are real and weighty. Thus for Murdoch the goodness of the good is available to us. But at the same time the reality of our complicity with the pain, suffering, and injustice suffusing reality, and the reality of our willful wrongdoing and culpability, can never be escaped or overcome. This is, to be sure, an improvement over the Nietzschean eliding of moral reality. But for Murdoch our lives are ultimately and *irredeemably* a mixture of good and evil, and thus the best we can do is struggle to orient our desires toward what is good and away from what is evil. We never, however, escape our guilt within Murdoch's eye-for-an-eye ethical economy.

Speaking technically for a moment, let me note that this same conceptual dead end also short-circuits Murdoch's final major work of philosophy, *Metaphysics as a Guide to Morals*, where she struggles admirably to rehabilitate the reality of the moral but remains finally within the grip of devastating modern conceptualities.[9] In particular, Murdoch views the atomistic, intentional self as basic, and is thus able to affirm eros but unable to envision full-fledged agape. As a result, she is at a loss when she finally confronts the spiritual challenge of affirmation posed by the reality of evil in her penultimate chapter, "Void." When in the closing pages of her argument she strives to articulate a beginning point for metaphysical reflection she is likewise at a loss. Tellingly, she affirms an "internal relation between truth and goodness and knowledge" but, unable to conceive of a beginning for these three, she imagines that in place of a beginning the best one can do is imagine some sort of mutually supporting circular relation among them.[10] Absent from Murdoch's thinking is love in the agapic, passive sense of the having been seized, which is the true "beginning" of morality and the ground of spiritual (in contrast to empirical or logical) truth, goodness, and knowledge.

Because Murdoch remains ensnared within neo-Nietzschean conceptual parameters, the Effingham Cooper example remains confusedly within the boundaries of aesthetic decentering and devastatingly devoid of the Faces of any

9. Iris Murdoch, *Metaphysics as a Guide to Morals* (New York: Penguin Books, 1993).
10. Ibid., 511.

others. As a result, what remains undeveloped are the dynamics of the having been seized that allow us, eyes wide open to all the evil, fully to release ourselves to the glory of a primordial and ultimate "yes" to reality, to others, and to ourselves without denial and without condemnation. Happily, as I will detail in conversation with Fyodor Dostoevsky's *The Brothers Karamazov*, on the far side of having been seized in and by love for all Faces we can live an eyes wide open "yes" to reality, to others, and to ourselves without denial and without condemnation.

AGAPE (THE MORAL) AND EROS (THE AESTHETIC)

On the far side of full-fledged affirmation of the moral as a function of love in the agapic sense, space opens up for discrete, full-fledged affirmation *of the aesthetic* as a manifestation of love in an unmitigated, full-bodied eros sense: namely, in the sense of what I desire for myself, desire for the sake of my own pleasure and delight. I have no need to make any attempt to smuggle morality and ethics into understanding that is constrained by the boundaries of the aesthetic sphere. Full-bodied affirmation of and respect for the priority and integrity of the moral, of agape, allows for full-bodied affirmation of the aesthetic, of eros.

In other words, since on this neo-Levinasian understanding we are not driven to try to salvage some simulacra of the ethical by turning it into a species of the aesthetic, we are freed to full-bodied affirmation of personal desires that do not violate any other Face, we are freed to full-bodied affirmation of delights enjoyed by and for our own Faces. For we each receive our own Faces as gifts, the latter Face in the Face to Face, and thus affirming delight for our own Faces is for ourselves, but not selfish. Insofar as eros does not violate agape—that is, insofar as my delight does not come at the expense of the violation of another's Face—both agape and also eros should be fully affirmed and celebrated.

In her theoretical understanding—though perhaps not in her real living—an eyes wide open "yes" to ourselves is beyond Murdoch's grasp. This is the devastating consequence of Murdoch's unwitting eliding of the moral, the devastating consequence of her attempt to bring back what she takes to be the essence of agape within aesthetic boundaries. Sadly, as will become increasingly clear, Murdoch remains cut off from an eyes wide open "yes" to ourselves. For when she elides the moral realm, she cuts herself off from having been seized in and by love for Faces. As a result she remains unwittingly and devastatingly cut off—in her theory, not necessarily in her life—from life awakened to having forgiven and having been forgiven, from the life of faith, from awakened surrender that provides affirmation of reality, of others, and of ourselves eyes wide open to evil (including our own complicity and culpability).

Chapter 8

Awakening in Dostoevsky
Markel and The Brothers Karamazov

MARKEL, ZOSIMA, ALYOSHA

". . . life is paradise, and we are all in paradise, but we do not want to know it . . . verily each one of us is guilty before everyone, for everyone and everything . . . how could we have lived before, getting angry, and not knowing anything?" Thus he awoke every day with more and more tenderness, rejoicing and all atremble with love . . . our garden was very shady, with old trees, the spring buds were already swelling on the branches, the early birds arrived, chattering and singing through his windows. And suddenly, looking at them and admiring them, he began to ask their forgiveness too: "Birds of God, joyful birds, you, too, must forgive me, because I have also sinned before you." None of us could understand it then, but he was weeping with joy: "Yes," he said, "there was so much of God's glory around me: birds, trees, meadows, sky, and I alone lived in shame, I alone dishonored everything, and I did not notice the beauty and glory of it all." "You take too many sins upon yourself," mother used to weep. "Dear mother, my joy, I am weeping from gladness, not from grief, I want to be guilty before them, only I cannot explain it to you, for I do not even know how to love

101

them. Let me be sinful before everyone, but so that everyone will forgive me, and that is paradise. Am I not in paradise now?[1]

This is the testimony of Markel, the mustard seed at the spiritual heart and narrative turning point of Fyodor Dostoevsky's *The Brothers Karamazov*. Often neglected, Markel's story takes up just four sparkling pages in the seven-hundred-plus page novel. Before the appearance of Markel, Dostoevsky has built up the modern Western case against Christianity (and faith in God generally) with incredible power. Far better known is a character whose understanding contrasts utterly with Markel's, Dostoevsky's antagonist, Ivan Karamazov. Ivan is the subject of the famous chapter, "Rebellion," and, in the novel, is the author of an equally famous story, "The Grand Inquisitor."

Ivan is educated in Europe and is clearly Dostoevsky's stand-in for modern Western rationality. Ivan overtly declares his primordial and ultimate belief in the power of "the Karamazov force . . . the force of the Karamazov baseness," which, in accord with predominant streams of modern Western rationality, is essentially a way of proclaiming that a drive to survive, the logic of domination, a logic of selfishness, enlightened or otherwise, is primordial and ultimate.[2] With Ivan, and culminating with his monumental "Rebellion" and "Grand Inquisitor" chapters, Dostoevsky gives powerful voice to modern Western rationality's passionate, ethical rejection of faith in God. Ivan's Western education facilitates his apparently brilliant arguments in "Rebellion" and "The Grand Inquisitor," and so he easily defeats the simplistic protests of his younger brother, Alyosha Karamazov, a youthful novice at the monastery.

Indeed, in a note, "From the Author," Dostoevsky openly worries that Ivan's arguments are so powerful that many readers will finish the book thinking Ivan's arguments are the most convincing. Dostoevsky proclaims Alyosha the "hero" of his novel, but he "decidedly doubts" he will "succeed in proving it to the reader."[3] Dostoevsky expects readers to find Alyosha to be "a strange man, even an odd one."[4] But Dostoevsky himself has no doubt that Alyosha is indeed the hero of *The Brothers Karamazov*. The problem, Dostoevsky suggests, is not with Alyosha, but with the modern milieu. For Alyosha will seem "odd" only because he is the sort of man who "bears within himself the heart of the whole, while the other people of his epoch have all for some reason been torn away from it for a time by some kind of flooding wind."[5] By the end of the novel Ivan is in a coma, his "Karamazov force" shattered by newborn awareness of complicity and culpability. The "Karamazov, we love you!" and "Hurrah for Karamazov!"

1. Fyodor Dostoevsky, *The Brothers Karamazov: A Novel in Four Parts with Epilogue*, trans. Richard Pevear and Larissa Volokhonsky (New York: Vintage Classics, 1991), 289–90.
2. Ibid., 263.
3. Ibid., 3.
4. Ibid.
5. Ibid.

repeated in the final paragraphs and lines of the novel are directed not to Ivan, but to the spirit of his now awakened and seasoned brother, Alyosha.[6]

As a young man, Alyosha had entered the monastery and become the disciple of its renowned elder, Zosima, "to whom he became attached with all the ardent first love of his unquenchable heart."[7] Alyosha, Dostoevsky's narrator specifies, was neither a fanatic nor a mystic, but entered the monastery because this path was "an ideal way out for his soul struggling from the darkness of worldly wickedness towards the light of love."[8]

Like Alyosha, Elder Zosima was no fanatic and no mystic. When he was young a seed of awakening had been sowed in Zosima by someone who had himself been newly awakened, his older brother, Markel, whose words open this chapter. Markel was a self-absorbed and irreligious boy who was struck down by disease in his youth. In the last weeks of his life Markel awakened to having been seized in and by love for all Faces, and he began to live the joy of having forgiven and having been forgiven. Zosima remembers Markel on his deathbed, when he was clearly seized in and by love for Zosima's Face:

> He beckoned me when he saw me, I went over to him, he took me by the shoulders with both hands, looked tenderly, lovingly into my face; he did not say anything, he simply looked at me like that for about a minute: "Well," he said, "go now, play, live for me!" . . . He died in the third week after Easter, conscious, and though he had already stopped speaking, he did not change to his very last hour: he looked joyfully, with gladness in his eyes, seeking us with his eyes, smiling to us, calling us . . . . It all shook me then, but not deeply, though I cried very much when he was buried. I was young, a child, but it all remained indelibly in my heart, the feeling was hidden there. It all had to rise up and respond in due time. And so it did.[9]

As a young adult, Zosima had gone some way toward establishing himself in the world as an up-and-coming military officer, living quite successfully the way of Ivan's "Karamazov force." His awakening was not gradual. He was smitten with a woman who was engaged to another man. Zosima deliberately maneuvered the man into a duel with pistols. On the evening before the duel, he arbitrarily and viciously beat his own servant, Alfanasy. The morning of the duel he woke up at the break of dawn, some hours before the appointed time. He opened the window "and looked into the garden—I watched the sun rising, the weather was warm, beautiful, the birds began to chime."[10] Suddenly, his beating of Alfanasy replayed through his mind, "What a crime! It was as if a sharp needle went through my soul . . . the sun was shining, the leaves were rejoicing, glistening,

6. Ibid., 775–76.
7. Ibid., 18.
8. Ibid.
9. Ibid., 290.
10. Ibid., 297.

and the birds, the birds were praising God . . . I covered my face with my hands, fell on my bed, and burst into sobs."[11]

Then Zosima remembered Markel's words, "truly each of us is guilty before everyone and for everyone, only people do not know it, and if they knew it, the world would at once become paradise."[12] "Lord," Zosima thinks, "can that possibly be true? Indeed, I am perhaps the most guilty of all, and the worst of all men in the world as well!"[13] And with the dawning of utter conviction over his guilt, over his complicity and culpability, Zosima received not condemnation but release and peace, for "suddenly the whole truth" appeared to him "in its full enlightenment."[14]

All that we read about Markel comes to us through Alyosha, who shares the tale of Markel with us just as Elder Zosima had shared it with him. Alyosha's own awakening, which takes place, note well, *after* the encounter with Ivan recounted in the "Rebellion" and "Grand Inquisitor" chapters, is more complex than Zosima's and is traced over the course of several chapters. The culminating moment comes in a period of crisis after the death of Zosima. While the Gospel lesson is being read over the coffin of Zosima, Alyosha, caught up in emotional and mental disequilibrium, stops listening, turns and walks out of the service. "Over him the heavenly dome, full of quiet, shining stars, hung boundlessly. . . the silence of the earth seemed to merge with the silence of the heavens . . . Alyosha stood gazing and suddenly, as if he had been cut down, threw himself to the earth."[15] He "did not know why he was embracing it, he did not try to understand why he longed so irresistibly to kiss it, to kiss all of it, but he was kissing it . . . and he vowed ecstatically to love it, to love it unto ages of ages."[16] Alyosha was rapturous, "He wanted to forgive everyone and for everything, and to ask forgiveness, oh, not for himself! but for all and for everything, 'as others are asking for me,' rang again in his soul."[17]

Alyosha, says the narrator, "fell to the earth a weak youth and rose up a fighter, steadfast for the rest of his life, and he knew it and felt it suddenly, in that very moment of his ecstasy. Never, never in all his life would Alyosha forget that moment, 'Someone visited my soul in that hour,' he would say afterwards, with firm belief in his words . . . ."[18]

Let me digress momentarily and note that it is unsurprising that Alyosha, having been seized in and by love for all Faces, and realizing the ecstasy of living beloved, living having forgiven and having been forgiven, characterizes this reality/dynamic in terms of the action of a person ("*Someone* visited my soul"). Given the power of having been seized in and by love for all Faces, and given

11. Ibid., 298.
12. Ibid.
13. Ibid.
14. Ibid.
15. Ibid., 362.
16. Ibid.
17. Ibid., 362–63.
18. Ibid., 363 (emphasis mine).

that the dynamics of having been seized make us aware that this love is not a product of our own intention, initiative, or action, and considering that our experiences of being loved are typically associated with the love of some other Face for us, the urge to personify the dynamic of having been seized is almost irresistible.

It is possible that there is something like an agent behind the love (e.g., a personal God). While that is certainly possible, however, the reality of having been seized in and by love does not include within itself a sufficient basis for inferring that an agent is the source of the love of the having been seized. Whatever one's final conviction or hope with regard to the question of some possible source of the love, however, the reality and character of the having been seized in and by love for all Faces, that is, the reality of agape, is beyond question.

In sum, Elder Zosima is the famed "Russian Monk," and Alyosha is the "hero" of *The Brothers Karamazov*, and their stories fill hundreds of its pages, but the one whose witness proves decisive in opening them to awakening is Markel. As Richard Pevear says in the introduction to his and Larissa Volokhonsky's translation of the novel, "Alyosha is saved at his darkest moment by his memory of the elder Zosima's voice, as Zosima was saved by the memory of his brother's voice. At the end of the novel, in his 'Speech at the Stone,' Alyosha hopes to pass this saving word on to the schoolboys."[19] It is curious that Pevear does not explicitly name Markel, for it is Markel's voice that Zosima hears, and the words that Alyosha remembers the elder Zosima giving voice are Markel's words. So, again, while the "hero" of the novel is Alyosha, and while Zosima is the renowned font of spiritual wisdom, the proximate source of this trajectory of awakening is Markel.

Markel is the figure through whom the revelation of agape shines with crystalline purity. The revelation of Markel stands at the heart of Dostoevsky's spiritual reply to the modern Western ethical rejection of faith in the divine, a rejection voiced powerfully through Ivan. After sharing the revelation by which Markel finds himself gloriously seized, Dostoevsky turns to unfold in realistic detail permutations of the same awakening as it manifests itself in diverse, complicated, and inevitably compromised ways in the lives of an array of characters—Elder Zosima, a "mysterious visitor," and Alyosha, among others— whose lives remain thoroughly inscribed in this vale of tears. Markel, too, lives still in this vale of tears, but his physical incapacity and nearness to death so free him from the burdens and compromises of this world that the reality of his awakening is manifest in rarified form. As a result, Dostoevsky is able to use

---

19. Richard Pevear, "Introduction," in Dostoevsky's *Brothers Karamazov*, xviii. Pevear, in contrast to the interpretation I am advancing, considers "memory" itself to be the "motif of this final episode." I am focused on the content and spirit communicated by the living and awakening voicing of the memory, an event of having been seized to which the "saving word" can help to awaken us. As a side note, Pevear's highlighting of Dostoevsky's experiences as a political prisoner, and of the terrifying mock execution that he endured, are very suggestive in relation to my interpretation.

Markel to draw a highly refined, concise, and radiant picture of awakening, of having been seized in and by love for all Faces.

To be clear, neither Dostoevsky nor Murdoch romanticize death. But they agree with the common idea that the near horizon of one's own death can stimulate special insight ("*can*," for there is nothing automatic or universal here). Now let me pause to be very precise. I am speaking of a very discrete and often very short interval of utter acceptance of imminent and unavoidable death. This interval arrives when you have moved beyond the mutually co-dependent poles of the dyad hope/anxiety. As long as the possibility of recovery/escape/survival remains in play, then struggle and the mutually co-dependent dyad hope/anxiety, and so perhaps even heightened concern for self and one's own survival, typically and appropriately remain in play.

Both Effingham and Ivan, however, enter that interval where you have reasonable, utter, and clear conviction over your own inevitable and imminent death, and in that interval you can experience a certain anticipatory "death of the self" that can be illuminating. (Though at first it seems paradoxical, the loss of all hope for one's survival brings with it the vanishing of all anxiety over one's death. More on this in chapter 10).[20] As was the case with Effingham Cooper, the near horizon of unavoidable death has served as a critical stimulus and awakened the formerly brash and arrogant Markel from self-incurved stupor. Beyond that, however, Dostoevsky and Murdoch differ profoundly about the character of the insight that can come in that interval.[21]

EFFINGHAM COOPER: AN AWFUL EITHER-OR

Murdoch imagined Effingham to have been awakened to a "love which was the same as death," the "death of the self" which makes "the world . . . quite automatically the object of a perfect love." As with Effingham, the proximity of death displaces Markel's self from the center of his notice. And like Effingham, Markel realizes that he has lived in profound isolation, realizes that he has been utterly self-incurved ("I alone . . . I alone . . . did not notice the beauty and glory of it all"). Markel, then, could partly agree with Effingham's contention that, "Before the self vanishes nothing really is . . . But as soon as the self vanishes everything is, and becomes automatically the object of perfect love."[22]

But whereas Murdoch imagines Effingham to have been awakened only to an "object," the "world," in such a fashion that no new self is reborn on the far side of the "death of the self" that Effingham undergoes, Dostoevsky imagines Markel to have been awakened to a world full of faces and Faces, the trees, the birds, family and friends, and also (implicit but clear in Markel's joy and

---

20. Here again the absence of debilitating physical or psychological trauma is prerequisite.
21. As Zosima and Alyosha, among many others, illustrate, other life events can stimulate the same insight.
22. Murdoch, *Unicorn*, 173.

delight) indirectly but decisively to his own beloved Face. Markedly absent from Effingham's awareness are any of the Faces that surround him in that bog (i.e., all the flora and fauna), or any memory of the Faces who have filled his life, let alone any awakening to having been seized in and by love for those Faces and awakening to his own Face as beloved.

Sadly, with the death of his self, Effingham *is not awakened in and by love for any Faces*. Effingham escapes his self-incurvature but is newly opened only to "a simple sum," to every*thing* that is not himself. Murdoch remains caught up in the "flooding wind" of modern Western rationality, and so when she imagines Effingham in the culminating moment of crisis, when he temporarily dies to his own self, she portrays him seeing not Faces but an object, "everything else." The absence of Faces in Effingham's vision protects him from condemnation because it protects him from moral reality and so from acknowledgment of his complicity and culpability (an instance of the modern Western evasion of the spiritual challenge of evil). But the price of this protection is monumental, for Effingham remains cut off from the joy of having been seized in and by love for other Faces, cut off from the joy of living in the light of having forgiven and having been forgiven, cut off from his own Face, cut off from the transcending joy of mutual, Face to Face communion, and so cut off from the paradise of "yes."

Insofar as Effingham is never awakened, it would seem natural to describe his condition, and the condition of others swept away in the same "flooding wind" as "asleep." But "asleep" is too pleasant a term to describe the awful condition of faces that are dead to all Faces (including their own Faces). "Self-incurved" or "primordially and ultimately self-concerned" are more descriptive but too dry to capture the unquenchable striving and, simultaneously, the anomie (i.e., listlessness, meaninglessness, emptiness) of such life, that is, of the life of faces that are dead to all Faces, the life of faces dead even to their own Faces, the life of faces caught up in a sort of living death.

Insofar as these are faces living devoid of awareness of their own or others' Faces, insofar as they are cognizant only of *thingly* reality, insofar as they are subject simultaneously to unquenchable striving and to anomie, and are in this sense living but dead, the living dead, it would be apt to call them "zombies." Perhaps part of what resonates in "zombie" movies is a justifiable and collective suspicion that we are surrounded by zombies, or perhaps even a lurking fear that we ourselves might largely be zombies. If so, we would discern here popular culture's collective affirmation of the contention that predominant forms of modern Western rationality have profoundly alienated us from life.

But "zombie" is too alienating a term, and too forgetful of the hidden but nonetheless real and abiding call of all Faces. "Zombie" should remain in the back of our minds, but it is also accurate and far more loving to use the traditional religious term "lost" to describe such faces, for "lost" conveys a sense of heart-wrenching poignancy and concern—the lost dog, the lost cat, the lost child—and "lost" can convey a real sense for the possibility of return, of being found, of reunion. So, we would say, sadly, awfully, Effingham Cooper is lost—but the possibility of awakening remains as long as his life endures.

The complete absence of Faces in Effingham's experience is devastating because it cuts him off from the paradise of surrender to having been seized in and by love. Given the ethical weight of moral reality in this vale of tears, however, and in particular the reality of our complicity and culpability, *from the perspective of those not awakened it seems desirable to be cut off from Faces.* For, as detailed above in relation to the fearsome horrors of this world, it is understandable that insofar as we are not awakened we strive to avoid the light of moral reality because we fear it will bring unbearable condemnation. As we have seen, Nietzsche gave brilliant expression to this dynamic of a morally motivated struggle to elide the reality of the moral. Precisely because of his profound moral sense for the unbearable and inescapable judgment he thinks affirmation of moral reality will bring down on us, Nietzsche strove to eliminate the moral altogether by transvaluing our values, that is, by wholly eliding the moral dimension of reality and replacing it with an aesthetic will to power.

At this juncture the full import of the disjunction between most of *The Unicorn*, where Murdoch—by illuminating the real and enduring ethical weight of moral reality—is concerned to oppose any Nietzschean eliding of the moral, and the experience of Effingham, which is beyond both ethical condemnation and moral awakening because it is utterly Faceless, becomes clear. With no place for love (agape) or forgiveness, Murdoch, like Nietzsche, is left with an awful either-or: *either* a realm of Faces where the full weight of ethical reality is in play, where we all are complicit and culpable and the best "yes" to ourselves that we can manage will depend on a hackneyed combination of inattention, scapegoating, and denial *or*, wholesale eliding of the realm of Faces, and so wholesale eliding of the moral, which involves, without rebirth, the "death of the self."[23]

Despite her struggles against Nietzsche, then, Murdoch finally remains caught within the same modern Western conceptual parameters that ensnared Nietzsche, and so she too pictures salvation at best in terms of a sort of transvaluation of values, in terms of a sphere wherein Faces (one's own and all others') and thereby the moral/ethical dimensions of reality are elided, and wherein we are invited to celebrate the otherness of a Faceless, thingly sphere.

In sum, Murdoch leaves Effingham in a spiritually/existentially untenable position. On the one hand, contra Nietzsche, she affirms moral reality, and describes inattention, scapegoating, and denial as a hackneyed group of coping mechanisms we use in order to escape being paralyzed by the condemnation that

---

23. This either-or in Murdoch differs from, but is reminiscent of and arguably complementary to, Taylor's "dilemma of mutilation"—the either-or between affirming our most profound moral convictions, which immediately turn in our hands and condemn us or, following Nietzsche, extirpating our most profound moral convictions, which is a form of spiritual mutilation (Charles Taylor, *Sources of the Self: The Making of the Modern Identity* [Cambridge: Harvard University Press, 1989], 520).

our complicity and culpability would otherwise immediately and devastatingly bring down on us. On the other hand, there is escape from condemnation. In Nietzschean fashion, however, this escape comes in a radical reorientation in which the moral sphere, the sphere of Faces, is utterly displaced. It is an escape that can seem glorious insofar as we are freed from condemnation, but it is an escape that comes at a terrible price, for with the eliding of the moral realm comes the eliding of all Faces, including our own Faces, a death of the self without return.

Along Murdoch's neo-Nietzschean path to "salvation" there is no grace, no forgiveness, and no rehabilitation and affirmation of Faces. In the end, Murdoch leaves Effingham with an awful either-or between the Faceless, amoral realm of everything that is not Effingham's self (i.e., the death of his self) *or* his old unregenerate self. Unsurprisingly, then, in sharp contrast to Markel, Zosima, and Alyosha, Murdoch specifies that just after Effingham is rescued, *only hours* after his "awakening," his same old, unregenerate self has returned, and he continues coping with the ethical weight of moral reality through various degrees of inattention, denial, and scapegoating.

IVAN KARAMAZOV: AN AWFUL EITHER-OR

The reality decisively missing in Murdoch is the reality of agape. Since the reality of agape is missing, the reality of having forgiven and having been forgiven is also missing, and Murdoch is cut off from realizing that we are primordially and ultimately response-able, moral, good, and beloved Faces. The absence of all of these glorious realities marks the devastating grip of paradigmatically modern Western rationality on her thought. Not coincidentally, Dostoevsky makes it clear that Ivan is in a similar position. Indeed, Ivan is a variation on the quintessential and sad Nietzschean figure described in chapter 1, "Unwitting Evasion: Suffering and Righteous Rejection of God," in terms of those who condemn God in moral indignation, often in the wake of witnessing some horror, as a way of dealing with the horror. The protest absorbs the energy of our moral horror while masking the real and enduring challenge of affirming reality and ourselves. But the enduring reality of the spiritual challenge of affirmation in the face of evil becomes clear when, in the name of consistency, we dismiss the idea of God and find ourselves still confronted by the same horror.

Notably, Ivan cuts a different figure than most anguished people who, brokenhearted, curse and reject God. Such people are typically despairing, broken, pained, and anguished in the face of horror. Many people who are inclined to follow Ivan and reject God out of moral outrage will have trouble even reading through the horrors Ivan recounts as he builds his moral case against God. Especially since Dostoevsky draws the brutal accounts that Ivan recites from real newspapers and history books (they are not fictitious) it is impossible for morally sensitive people to read the "Rebellion" chapter without feeling anguish over the suffering and violence described (babies hoisted on bayonets, children nailed by the ears to walls, torn apart by dogs—the accounts are unbearable).

Of course, the power of Ivan's argument depends on the reader's moral horror. Moral readers will be overwhelmed with sorrow and anguish over the evil and suffering described. Over the course of the "Rebellion" chapter, however, it becomes clear that *Ivan is not overwhelmed by the evil and suffering.* Ivan is *empowered.* He even seems to be enjoying himself. This realization can seem surprising, since Ivan clearly intends his recitation of the accounts to generate genuine moral horror. But the sense of surprise dissipates when one remembers that Ivan is using this argument to defend his explicit embrace of the "Karamazov force . . . the force of the Karamazov baseness." What we stumble over here is an internal contradiction in Ivan's argument. For the argument pivots on affirmative use of precisely the moral reality and moral sensitivity that Ivan rejects in his affirmation of the Karamazov baseness. That is, Ivan's *quintessentially moral* argument is used to support an *affirmation of amorality.*

This is not merely a logical contradiction, nor is it one Ivan is self-consciously and deliberately foisting on his interlocutors. Ivan is no psychopath. He is neither amoral nor even especially immoral. To the contrary, his rejection of moral reality, like Nietzsche's, betrays incredible moral sensitivity. Like Nietzsche, Ivan senses inchoately but intensely that he will not be able to accept himself or reality if he owns his moral sensitivities. Moved by moral sensitivities he is desperate to disavow, Ivan launches a self-contradictory argument that depends on affirmative use of the moral in the course of rejecting the moral. Once noted, the contradiction is obvious, but Ivan unwittingly masks it ("unwittingly" because he masks it both from himself and from his interlocutors) with a deception (and a self-deception) that, while subtle, is so manifestly false that we might call it delusional.

A skillful rhetorician, Ivan leads with overt claims over which he correctly expects agreement. Ivan recites a dramatic, painful litany of moral horrors. Indeed, we are horrified. In reply to the youthful Alyosha's wooden appeals to Christian doctrine, Ivan rejects any calculus that would claim to make right or excuse the horrors. In particular, he rejects tit-for-tat economies, including the idea that any future punishment, sacrifice, or great good could undo, justify, or redeem the horrors. In this vein Ivan ridicules Alyosha's idea that killing an innocent man, or God killing himself [i.e., the Son], can somehow, tit-for-tat, undo, justify, or redeem the evil of the torture of those children. Again, the morally sensitive should agree with Ivan's criticism of Alyosha (though we should not be impressed by the youthful Alyosha's understanding of Christian doctrine). On all these points, which reflect real moral sensitivity, we should be in passionate agreement with Ivan.

But then, like a skillful magician, Ivan misdirects our attention with a dazzling distraction. Ivan declares passionately that even if God does exist, he hands God back his (i.e., Ivan's) ticket to this creation, for the suffering of even one whimpering child is too steep, too morally repugnant a price to pay.[24] Here again, leaving aside Ivan's primitive understanding of "God," we concur with his rejection of any such tit-for-tat exchange (e.g., that I would be willing to gain my existence at the cost of that child's suffering), and we continue to be confirmed by and affirming of Ivan's ethical passion. But amidst all the moral agreement and fireworks over rejecting God's world and giving back one's ticket, it is easy to miss the subtle but sure way in which Ivan writes himself, and by proxy those who might be tempted to follow him all the way to the rejection of God, off the moral page.

Ivan declares this world morally unacceptable and hands back his ticket to God as if he exists in splendid isolation, as if he is not himself a part of this world, as if he is not by virtue of his very existence complicit in all the evil, as if he has never been culpable of any intentional wrongdoing, as if his highly moral blaming of God deflects any and all moral complicity and blame away from himself, indeed, as if his handing back of his "ticket" is an act of righteous independence, as if, to put it bluntly and so make the delusion obvious, as if he and, by proxy, those who agree with him, are perfectly innocent, ethically blameless, utterly autonomous and self-subsistent, in no way complicit with the horrors suffusing reality. Remember too the contradiction: he advances this whole moral but deluded argument in defense of his overt embrace of the "Karamazov force . . . the force of the Karamazov baseness."

Ivan presents himself and is seen by others as strong and confident. But since his existential position is delusional (for he is not radically autonomous, self-subsistent, and innocent) and self-contradictory (for he both affirms and rejects the moral), Ivan's existential position is actually quite precarious. Since Ivan does indeed exist as a part of this vale of tears, and since moral reality is indeed real, and since Ivan actually is intensely morally sensitive, Ivan's denial and delusion collapse as life inexorably brings home the reality of his own ethical complicity and culpability.

Sadly, the weight of his complicity and culpability is brought home while Ivan remains committed to his own autonomy and his will to wholly autonomous self-affirmation. With the loss of delusion and denial, with intense moral sensitivity, but without awakening, without having been seized in and by love, without living in the light of having forgiven and having been forgiven, Ivan is left with nothing but crushing self-condemnation.

Notably, Ivan evidences far greater ethical integrity and intensity than Effingham, who quickly morphs back into his old, unregenerate self and gets back to muddling through life with inattention, denial, and scapegoating. Ivan, sadly but to his credit, maintains his ethical integrity and intensity even after the delusion is pierced and his complicity and culpability are forcefully brought home. With the loss of delusion, with full moral sensitivity, but still hardened against having been seized in and by love, and thus with no openness to having

24. Dostoevsky, *Brothers Karamazov*, 244–46.

forgiven or having been forgiven, Ivan is left with nothing but crushing ethical self-condemnation. By novel's end, accordingly, the "Karamazov" of the awakened Alyosha is heralded while Ivan, Dostoevsky's stand-in for modern Western rationality, his delusion of innocence and self-subsistence rent by reality, "lives" on in a coma.

In direct contrast to the tragic figure of Ivan, the blazing significance of Markel shows forth with saving intensity. Let me now turn back to Markel's awakening and detail the essential dynamics—the dynamics of agape— that end up saving Dostoevsky's intended hero of the novel, Alyosha.

Chapter 9

Joy Eyes Wide Open to Evil

Grace and the Paradise of "Yes"

EYES WIDE OPEN

In Markel, Dostoevsky offers us a stark contrast to the two variations of modern Western lostness represented by Effingham and Ivan. Having been seized in and by love for the Faces of all creatures, new horizons of meaningfulness and joy explode into Markel's awareness. He is awakened to the joy of having been seized in and by love for the Faces of all the creatures that surround him (his mother, his brother, the servants, the birds, the budding trees), he is released into the freedom of living having forgiven and having been forgiven, and he is released to carefree delight in creation (the beauty of other creatures, the meadows, the sky).

There is no denial of evil in Markel. For to be awakened to the moral dimension of reality means not only joy, forgiveness, and carefree delight but also living eyes wide open to all the pain, suffering, and injustice afflicting Faces, and living eyes wide open to one's own complicity and culpability. Dostoevsky makes this point decisively with Markel's astounding assertion that "verily each one of us is guilty before anyone, for everyone and everything." The astounding severity of this assertion becomes clear when we realize that each one of us should hear it like this: "I, *I* am more guilty than anyone else, *I* am guilty for

113

everyone else's wrongdoing, *I* am guilty for all the evil suffusing the world." (Is a more stark contrast to Ivan's self-righteousness imaginable?) Remember that this is how Zosima at the critical moment owned Markel's insight: "Indeed, I am perhaps the most guilty of all, and the worst of all men in the world as well!"[1] It can, however, be very easy to miss Markel's meaning.

First, let me be quick to stress that Markel's astounding assertion is not ethical. Ethically his assertion is obviously false: Markel is not guilty for all the wrongdoing in the world. Indeed, let us digress momentarily to reiterate that we never forget ethical realities, we never forget which faces are culpable, and nothing in our position commends any passivity, any failure to discern wrongdoing, any failure to act decisively, perhaps even violently in defense of what is good and just in the realm of faces. But neither, as we have also stressed, do we ever forget any Faces, or forget that moral reality, the reality of gracious love, is primordial and ultimate. The realm of Faces, the realm of the moral, is precisely the realm from which Markel is making this astounding assertion, which is thereby not finally ethical but moral. The assertion, then, is definitively shaped not only by recognition of complicity and culpability but, decisively, by awakening to having been seized in and by love for all Faces.

Markel is difficult to understand because he is testifying from the supra-ethical, moral perspective of those who are awakened; he is testifying to the release and peace of living having forgiven and having been forgiven. His is testimony offered in the light of a reality and realm that transcends and definitively qualifies the ethical. There is, then, a fundamental shift in the framing perspective in play, such that Markel's assertion will be unintelligible insofar as one is not awakened.

Significantly, as Dostoevsky feared, those conditioned by predominant forms of modern Western rationality are likely to find *Ivan's* way of thinking far more resonant than Markel's. Indeed, there is a very real risk that those who think within a modern Western framework will fail to discern that Ivan's position is self-contradictory and deluded. In any case, because Markel is testifying from the far side of complete release to having been seized in and by love for all Faces, because he is testifying to how reality looks when you live total surrender to having been seized in and by love, that is, because he is testifying to how reality looks when you live total surrender to faith in God, he literally cannot be understood insofar as you think from the perspective of the logic of domination (i.e., from the perspective of the atomistic "I"). Insofar as you remain captive to the logic of domination, Markel will seem enigmatic at best and pathologically self-despising at worst.

But there is nothing pathetic, pathological, or self-despising about Markel proclaiming, "I want to be guilty before them," or, "Let me be sinful before

---

1. Fyodor Dostoevsky, *The Brothers Karamazov: A Novel in Four Parts with Epilogue*, trans. Richard Pevear and Larissa Volokhonsky (New York: Vintage Classics, 1991), 298.

everyone."[2] To the contrary, what is really visible in his seemingly self-destructive desire personally to own guilt "before anyone," "for everyone," and "for everything" is the wondrous, spiraling dynamic between the joy of living having forgiven and having been forgiven and a desire to confess all the more completely, since confession frees one ever more fully to the reality of having forgiven and having been forgiven. Markel lives in the light of having been seized in and by love for all Faces, and so he lives and wants to live eyes wide open to his own complicity and culpability, and, most especially, he wants to expose his complicity and culpability *and all* complicity and culpability to the expiating light of gracious love as completely as possible, and thus to live the full glory of having been forgiven for, and of having forgiven, *everything*: ". . . I want to be guilty before them, only I cannot explain it to you, for I do not even know how to love them. Let me be sinful before everyone, but so that everyone will forgive me, and that is paradise. Am I not in paradise now?"[3]

CONFESSION AND RELEASE

To the degree one owns complicity and culpability *apart* from awakening one is burdened by guilt. Effingham (inattention and scapegoating), Nietzsche (attempt to "self-overcome" the moral through a transvaluation of values), and Ivan (delusion and self-contradictory denial, then coma) illustrate various responses to the unexpiated burden of guilt.[4] And for those with intense moral sensitivity like Nietzsche and Ivan, the burden of and so the reaction to recognition of one's complicity and culpability apart from awakening can be especially intense. So it is wholly understandable that Nietzsche and others who struggle to affirm themselves recoil when confronted with their own complicity or culpability.

Confessing complicity and culpability in the light of having been seized, however, is radically different from recognizing complicity and culpability when one is struggling to establish, justify, and affirm oneself, that is, when one is still caught up in the atomistic I's futile struggle for wholly autonomous self-affirmation. For in stark contrast to the burden of recognition of guilt apart from awakening, confession in the light of having been seized is not finally a burden. To be sure, confession too involves recognition of guilt, and that recognition retains a real if transient burning character. Most significantly, however, confession occurs within the context of having been

---

2. Dostoevsky, *Brothers Karamazov*, 289–90. The "let me be" is in the passive voice because one does *not* own one's complicity and culpability *in order to* gain release.

3. Ibid., 289–90.

4. One could also interpret the suicide of Judas Iscariot as the depiction in the New Testament of a response along these lines, that is, as a response to overwhelming owning of complicity and culpability apart from awakening.

seized in and by love. And because the love in and by which you have been seized is gracious, confessing your complicity and culpability does not preeminently or finally bring condemnation. For insofar as one lives in the light of the having been seized, one lives always already having forgiven and having been forgiven.

Markel is not simply acknowledging guilt, Markel is *confessing*, and that explains his astounding assertion of ethical responsibility. Markel wants to be guilty "before anyone," "for everyone," and "for everything" not because he is self-hateful but because insofar as he exposes all complicity and culpability, all evil, everyone's wrongdoing to the light of "yes," he lives having forgiven and having been forgiven and so inhabits the paradise of "yes" all the more fully. Confession, again, is not a sign of having been overcome by guilt. Confession is a sign of surrender to having been seized in and by love within this vale of tears. Markel's confession, "I . . . before everyone . . . for everyone . . . for everything," names an astoundingly severe owning of ethical complicity and culpability while still living fully in the light of gracious love, in the light of a primordial and ultimate "yes."

Let me reiterate this paradoxical but vital point. Markel wants to be guilty "before anyone," "for everyone," and "for everything" not because he is self-hateful but because insofar as he exposes *all* complicity and culpability to the light of "yes," he lives the reality of having forgiven every Face (awakened or lost), and he lives the reality of having been forgiven, and so he inhabits the paradise of "yes" all the more fully. Insofar as he lives having forgiven everyone and having been forgiven for everything, he lives without condemnation or hatred of any others or of himself, he lives, through the power of the love of the having been seized, into the reality that *all* complicity, *all* culpability, *all* wrong is primordially and ultimately transcended in the "yes" of gracious love, and with his life and testimony he bears witness to the glorious, primordial, and ultimate reality that is a saving truth for all.

Insofar as we confess, we relinquish attempts at establishing ourselves, attempts at self-justification. Confession, then, marks and brings continuing success in living surrender to having been seized in and by love, and so it marks life increasingly lived having forgiven and having been forgiven. Markel's astoundingly severe assumption of guilt for all evil and all wrongdoing, then, is a sign not of confusion or self-hatred but a sign of awakening, a sign of the most wondrous, complete, and unmitigated confession and inhabiting of "yes" imaginable. That is why Markel's astoundingly severe owning of guilt for all evil delivers not crushing self-condemnation or shame but surpassing and resilient joy: "Thus he awoke every day with more and more tenderness, rejoicing and all atremble with love."[5]

5. Dostoevsky, *Brothers Karamazov*, 289.

THE DESOLATION OF DENIAL

A temptation that often manifests itself when we sense ourselves inextricably tied to complicity and culpability is denial. Ironically, as Nietzsche and Ivan illustrate, the existential energy behind denial can be the product not of indifference or immorality but, to the contrary, the product of burning moral sensitivity to your own complicity and culpability, a sensitivity that causes you to recoil from the slightest sense of complicity or culpability. Devastatingly, this self-interested, defensive denial keeps us focused on ourselves, obstructs awakening to having been seized in and by love for the Faces of others, and keeps our energies directed either toward devastating, self-enclosed, futile attempts to justify ourselves or toward the spiritual mutilation of Nietzschean transvaluation (i.e., defensive denial keeps one trapped within the either-or of self-condemnation or spiritual self-mutilation).

Paradoxically, frank acknowledgment of evil and of our own complicity and culpability does not bring condemnation to those who are morally awake, to those who are caught eyes wide open in this vale of tears, to those who are brutally honest about their own complicity and culpability. Indeed, condemnation is effectively a lived final word only for those who remain in denial over their complicity and culpability, who strive (futilely, tragically) to assert and establish themselves. For insofar as such poor Faces remain cut off from realization of the glory of having been seized in and by love, they remain lost to the devastating logic of domination, and they remain helplessly bound to the very complicity and culpability they strive so desperately and futilely to deny. Predominant streams of modern Western rationality, most especially those that systemically elide the moral dimension of reality, can function as an especially aggressive, if largely unwitting, manifestation of such devastating denial.

To the degree one's heart and mind is caught up in primordial affirmation of the atomistic "I," to the degree one sees oneself as fundamentally alone and in need of establishing oneself, letting go of self-assertion and releasing oneself to having been seized in and by love for the Faces of others can feel risky, even suicidal, like an absolute loss of self (so, says Markel, "we do not want to know it"). But what we can come to realize through reflection on the moral reality of having been seized in and by love for the Faces of others is that only to the degree we lessen our grip on self-assertion and open ourselves to the having been seized do we receive, indirectly but decisively, "yes" to our own Faces. For in reality my own "I" is not fundamental. My own "I" is not an atomistic starting point. My own "I" is not what I know most surely and most significantly.

We know ourselves most surely and assuredly in our having been seized in and by love for other Faces. That having been seized in and by love for other Faces is the event that is absolutely prior and originary. As is often surprisingly obvious on reflection, having been seized in and by love for other Faces is at the heart of the most meaningful, precious, and significant moments of our lives. While these are moments when we are seized primarily and most profoundly by the Faces of others, they are also precisely the moments when we truly receive ourselves, when we receive ourselves, indirectly but decisively, as blessed gifts, when we receive ourselves as Faces in our response-ability, when we receive ourselves as the second, also infinitely beloved Face in the Face to Face.

Denial of complicity and culpability cuts us off from such precious moments. To be precise, it is not the denial in and of itself that cuts us off from such precious moments, but the root and motivation of the denial, the existential stance from which it flows. For the existential stance at the root of denial is the stance of the atomistic I's will to power, will to self-affirmation, to self-assertion, a stance that cuts us off from having been seized in and by love. The existential stance of domination leads us to attempt to assert and establish ourselves over and against the whole world, to assert ourselves as primordial and ultimate. This self-assertion is meant to be salvific, to be a means by which we can save ourselves. It can feel deceptively empowering. Because it cuts us off from the "yes" of having been seized in and by love for the Faces of others, however, it is in reality a futile and devastatingly self-destructive effort, cutting us off from gracious love, from other Faces, even from our own Faces.

Emmanuel Levinas frequently quotes Pascal in this regard, "'That is my place in the sun.' That is how the usurpation of the whole world began."[6] Levinas thinks Pascal had already in the seventeenth century discerned the solipsistic, nihilistic usurpation of the whole world embedded at the heart of modern Western rationality (paradigmatically enshrined in Descartes's fateful "I think, therefore I am" and in the advent of epistemology as "first philosophy"). This is a rationality that conceptually closes us off from the "yes" of having been seized in and by love. Insofar as we idealize and pursue the modern I's delusory usurpation of the whole world (let alone embrace the totalizing empiricism of scientism), we spiritually annihilate ourselves, we usher ourselves into the desolation of denial, and we remain lost to the "yes" of having been seized in and by love for all Faces.[7]

By contrast, let me reiterate, Markel's astounding, unmitigated, total confession of guilt for all evil and all wrongdoing, far from being a mark of confusion or self-hatred, is a mark of the most wondrous, complete, and unmitigated inhabiting of the paradise of "yes" imaginable. It represents the complete opposite of Ivan's impossible effort at atomistic self-justification and self-affirmation, the complete opposite of "my place under the sun."

---

6. Emmanuel Levinas, *Otherwise Than Being, or Beyond Essence*, trans. Alphonso Lingis (Pittsburgh: Duquesne University Press, 1981), viii, citing Blaise Pascal, *Pensées*, trans. A. J. Krailsheimer (New York: Penguin Books, 1966), 47 (*la pensée* 64 in Krailsheimer and *la pensée* 295 in the Brunschvicg edition—Levinas cites it as *la pensée* 112).

7. Thus Levinas argues for ethics as first philosophy, that is, for taking awakening to agape as what is most basically and significantly given.

THE MIRACLE OF "YES"

Since awakening involves openness to the horrors of this vale of tears, and to one's own complicity and culpability, having forgiven and having been forgiveness are an aspect of all true awakening. Thus all of Markel, Zosima, and Alyosha's talk of guilt and forgiveness, talk that would be abhorrent to Nietzsche and Ivan and literally unthinkable within the Faceless conceptual parameters of Effingham's experience, is an essential aspect of their testimony. It is no accident, then, that radical confession and naming of the wondrous having forgiven and having been forgiven is so prominent in Markel's testimony and recurs, with complementary accents, at the heart of the testimonies of Zosima and Alyosha.

To reiterate, rapturous light dawned as Zosima, with the accent moving from "each of us" to "I," realized truly, "I am perhaps most guilty of all, and the worst of all men in the world as well!"[8] The same dynamic, with a gesture to the transcending joy of mutual, Face to Face communion, is evident in Alyosha at his own moment of transforming realization, "He wanted to forgive everyone and for everything, and to ask forgiveness, oh, not for himself! but for all and for everything, 'as others are asking for me,' rang again in his soul."[9]

The quote with which we opened this reflection on *The Brothers Karamazov*, Markel's proclamation that "life is paradise, and we are all in paradise . . ." testifies to a miracle. This, I think I can now conclude, is the miracle Charles Taylor gestured toward in his reference to a divine affirmation of the human, far greater than humans could ever attain unaided. For Markel's incredible confession of personal guilt—"each one of us is guilty before everyone, for everyone and everything"—brings not self-condemnation or shame, but surpassing and resilient joy: "Thus he awoke every day with more and more tenderness, rejoicing and all atremble with love." This portrays the miracle of the love of the having been seized. The love in and by which we have been seized is gracious, and so it involves utter owning of one's own complicity and culpability and, moreover, in a move that transcends and relativizes all evil, it involves utter owning of *all* complicity and culpability. It is precisely the astounding severity of this owning of all evil that reveals in fullness the transcending reality and power of grace and the saving character of the spiritual awakening that delivers us, eyes wide open in this vale of tears, not to despair and condemnation but to release, joy, and delight.[10]

Let me pause, however, and make explicit an obvious point about living in the paradise of "yes." Since we live on in this vale of tears, our complicity and

8. Dostoevsky, *Brothers Karamazov*, 298.
9. Ibid., 362 (emphasis mine).
10. Of course, we are talking in all of this about spiritual condemnation/self-condemnation (the ethical in the light of the moral), which is surpassingly significant. As Dostoevsky makes clear in the story of "the mysterious visitor," however, the consequences *within history* of full owning and public confession of ethical culpability for specific acts of evil (in the case of the mysterious visitor, for a murder) can be very significant (e.g., involving societal condemnation and legal punishment). Nonetheless, as Dostoevsky makes equally clear, the spiritual stakes remain transcendingly significant.

culpability are ever renewing, ongoing realities. We live always newly complicit and culpable, and we live always already having forgiven and having been forgiven. As long as our lives in this world endure there will be a continual dialectic between searing guilt and the release of living in the expiating light of the love of the having been seized, the release of living having forgiven and having been forgiven. However, in accord with the asymmetry between "yes" and "yes-violated," and despite the enduring dialectic between guilt and release, the relation is asymmetrical (the decisive asymmetry). What is preeminent and final is not guilt but release, the joy of awakening, that is, the joy of living in the light of the having been seized in and by love for every Face, the joy of living having forgiven and having been forgiven.

Notably, insofar as those who are awake and living in the light live the glorious release of having forgiven and having been forgiven, insofar as they have surrendered to love even for enemies of the moral, they will be overcome with grief over Faces deceived by the devastating idolizing of the atomistic I and the self-incurved drive to wholly autonomous self-affirmation. For such self-incurved faces have lost touch with all other Faces. And because they are not awake to having been seized in and by love for other Faces, they have lost touch with their own Faces. They are not awake to their response-ability, and they are not awake to the indirect but decisive way in which they too can know themselves as having been seized in and by infinite love. Such lost faces still bear the awful weight of complicity and culpability, and they are still cut off from the primordial, ultimate, and gracious "yes" that is always already proffered to them.

Such pitiable, cut-off, incurved faces, captives of the devastating logic of domination, do not deserve or need further judgment or condemnation. It is not confession that brings release but release that brings confession. The weight of our complicity and culpability is a given; it bears down on us from youth. So, again, there is no need to hammer home complicity and culpability and no help in doing so. The profound need of cut-off, self-incurved Faces is not accusation but awakening. They do not need to be overcome by guilt (as, for instance, Ivan was overcome by guilt) but by the gracious love of the having been seized. What comes first in the dynamic of awakening is not guilt but love, the gracious love of the having been seized, for confession is an honest acknowledgment of ethical responsibility that neither stems from nor, finally, delivers guilt, shame, or condemnation.

The absolute owning of all guilt in confession marks the moral transcending of evil through the work of the love of the having been seized, and because that is also the transcending of good-in-contrast-to-evil, that is, the transcending of the ethical sphere wherein good and evil, in concept and in reality, co-originate, confession marks life lived in the light of the sphere of the moral, the transcending sphere of love, which evil does not defeat (the asymmetry). Salvation from complicity and culpability, then, comes not through denial of the moral, not in denial of one's ethical complicity and culpability, but in radical, unmitigated awakening to the moral, and complete confession of *all* ethical complicity and culpability.

In sum, Markel bears witness to the character and joy of living in the paradise of "yes." He is awakened wholly to the Faces of all the creatures around him, and thus he is awakened not only to boundless vistas of joy and happiness, he is awakened with full intensity to all the pain, suffering, evil, hatred, and injustice suffusing reality, and to his own complicity and culpability. But he is awakened to all of this in the light of the love of the having been seized. Because he has been seized in and by love, he has abandoned all attempts at self-assertion, at self-justification, he has moved beyond all denial, and because he has opened himself to all of the pain, suffering, and injustice of the world not only without denial or mitigation but with astounding confession of complicity and culpability in and with all of it, he lives released from condemnation of others and of reality, and released from condemnation of himself.

Facing imminent death in this vale of tears, eyes wide open to his own total complicity and culpability, eyes wide open to all the evil suffusing reality, Markel is not overwhelmed nor in the slightest shaken by "no." He is overwhelmed with joy and delight, for he has been seized in and by love for all Faces, including his own, he lives having forgiven everything and having been forgiven for everything, he lives in the expiating light of a primordial and ultimate affirmation, and so he lives rejoicing in the paradise of "yes." Gloriously awakened, having been seized in and by love for the Faces of all the faces that surround him, the Faces of trees, birds, and people, and surrounded by brilliant, delightful, meaningful life, love, and beauty, living in the light of total having forgiven and having been forgiven, Markel is carefree, delighted, marveling, joyful, rapturous: "am I not in paradise now?"

Chapter 10

Death's Gift to Life

Living Now Eternally

A GIFT OF DEATH: THE CRITICAL INTERVAL

Since our existence, our life, is a gift, since it is not anything to which we can claim a right, such that it would be wrong if we had never existed, it is not clear that death in and of itself is evil. On the other hand, death, which to every appearance breaks utterly and forevermore all relation to all other Faces, which to every appearance marks the absolute end of joy and delight for the one who has died, which to every appearance marks the complete end of every Face, is most certainly not in itself a good to be pursued or celebrated. Death itself can become a relative good, but only in the context of circumstances so exceptional (e.g., where one might give one's life to save others) or suffering so horrible that dying becomes preferable to living. As Levinas says, death (or the dire circumstances that make death a relative good) always comes too soon.[1]

As both Murdoch and Dostoevsky realize, however, while death in and of itself is not a good to be pursued or celebrated, the near horizon of your own

1. Emmanuel Levinas, *Entre Nous: Thinking-of-the-Other*, trans. Michael Smith and Barbara Harshav (New York: Columbia University Press, 1998), 130.

unavoidable death can bring a powerful gift if you are caught up in the logic of domination and need not become an overwhelming source of grief for those who live awakened but facing imminent death (it is a source of grief but not a source of an *overwhelming* grief). I am speaking of a gift that typically comes in an interval that is discrete and often very short, and which is distinguished by complete and utter acceptance of imminent and unavoidable death. This interval constitutes a discrete and final horizon before unavoidable and impending death. It is an interval where you have moved utterly beyond hope for survival, where you secret no expectations of survival, none whatsoever, and thus where you have moved beyond any anxiety related to that hope.

People rightly experience considerable anxiety as they struggle to survive in the face of possible or likely death, that anxiety is indexed precisely to their hopes for survival, and in particular to fear that their hopes for survival may be thwarted. This particular hope and its correlate anxiety—namely, the anxiety that your hopes for survival are in vain—mutually co-originate and disappear entirely in that final interval, where you have neither hope for survival nor the correlate anxiety, for you have no doubt that your death is unavoidable and imminent. Ordinarily, hope and anxiety are appropriately and intensely indexed to concern for your own face and Face. But when you make the psychological quantum shift to that final, terminal interval before death, where any hope for your survival has completely and utterly died, and so *where all anxiety related to fear over that hope being thwarted has likewise died*, then concern for your own Face can rapidly fade.

In other words, if you make the quantum shift into that discrete interval where you have reasonable, total, clear, and utter conviction over the unavoidable reality of your own imminent death, and if you are free of debilitating physical or psychological impediments, then you can experience a certain anticipatory death of the "self" of the logic of domination, that is, a death of the self-incurved self, a death of the atomistic, autonomous modern self that thinks that it exists first and foremost over and against all other Faces. This death of that "self" can facilitate illumination insofar as it pierces or, in the case of those already awakened, purifies you of self-incurvature and frees you from the logic of domination. So opened or, for those already awakened, so opened all the more fully to the glory of having been seized in and by love for all the Faces that surround you, you are rapidly ushered into the paradise of "yes" through the dynamics of the having been seized.

Let me be clear that this final interval *should not* be in play if there is any possibility of recovery, escape, or survival. In that context the struggle to survive and the forces of anxiety and hope, and even heightened concern for self, all ordinarily and appropriately remain in play. But once you have entered that interval where the unavoidable and impending reality of your own death has rendered hope/struggle/anxiety over your own Face moot, then, since affirmation of your own Face flows not prior to but in and through your having been seized in and by love for all other Faces, including the host of Faces who will live on, your joy for those Faces remains vibrant (so Markel says, "go now, live, play for me"). Beyond the terror and anguish that may be a prior part of your final moments, you can find a transcending solace in the joy of having been seized in and by love for all the enduring Faces.

THE GIFT OF DEATH IN MURDOCH AND DOSTOEVSKY

Murdoch and Dostoevsky both realize that the near horizon of unavoidable death can work powerfully for awakening. In the cases of both Effingham and Markel, the near horizon of unavoidable death defeats self-incurvature and the logic of domination and stimulates new openness to what is other. As we have discussed, however, for Effingham as imagined by Murdoch, the revelation remains incomplete and ephemeral. Murdoch puts it this way, "Why had Effingham never realized that [death] was the only fact that mattered, perhaps the only fact there was? If one had realized this, one could have lived all one's life in the light." At this pivotal juncture, however, Murdoch's insightfulness falters, for death in and of itself is not the only fact that matters. Moreover, as we have noted, Murdoch fails to move beyond a series of abstractions (e.g., "being," "everything else") in unfolding the meaning and significance of "the light."

It is not death itself but the near horizon of your own imminent and unavoidable death that may shatter self-incurvature, that may dislodge the "I" of the logic of domination, that may displace what Murdoch calls Effingham's "old, unregenerate self." But to name only the death of the "I" of the logic of domination is to tell only half the story, for—and here we move beyond Murdoch decisively—the death of the "I" of domination is truly revelatory only when it leads to awakening, only when it opens you to having been seized in and by love for all Faces, including your own, only when it marks the birth of the "I" awakened to the paradise of "yes."

In stark contrast to Murdoch, we have barely discussed the dying of the old "I" because our attention is so profoundly and wondrously seized by awakening, by having been seized in and by love for all Faces. This is first and foremost an awakening to all other Faces. It is also, indirectly but decisively, an awakening to the gift of your own Face, the second but nonetheless infinitely beloved Face in the Face to Face. It is an awakening to the freedom of living having forgiven and having been forgiven, and thereby an avenue to innocent delight in all that is pleasing in creation (i.e., to eros enjoyed in the expiating light of having forgiven and having been forgiven). The truly profound gift of awareness of imminent and unavoidable death, then, is the shattering of self-incurvature, the falling-away of the scales that have obstructed our vision and cut us off from having been seized in and by love for the Faces of others, and so an opening to awakening and entrance into the glory of the paradise of "yes."

As we have seen, Dostoevsky portrays Markel's awakening in precisely this fashion. Markel enters that final, terminal interval. Full of vanity and youthful arrogance, Markel's self-incurvature is shattered by the near horizon of his own impending and unavoidable death. This gift of the death of his self-incurved self frees him from the logic of domination. He is awakened to having been seized in and by love for all Faces, including his own. He is awakened to the paradise of "yes." Markel knows full well he is about to die. But Markel, having been seized in and by love for all the Faces that surround him, the Faces of trees, birds, and people, released into life lived in the light of having forgiven and having been forgiven, Markel, marveling, joyful over all Faces, delighting in all creation, surrounded by brilliant, meaningful life, love, and beauty, Markel is rapturous: "am I not in paradise now?"

WARM COMFORT

Dostoevsky, who had lost his own beloved little girl shortly before writing *The Brothers Karamazov*, does not romanticize Markel's youthful death from disease. Yet Dostoevsky makes clear that Markel's sense for the gift of life and the glory of "yes" is so passionate and overwhelming that death, always a real loss to be mourned, loses its sting: "Why count the days, when even one day is enough for a man to know all happiness."[2] This statement illustrates the shift from the possessive, self-incurved logic of domination (the stance of one who would "count the days") to the stance of one who is taken up in the glory of having been seized in and by love for all Faces, the stance of one who receives every moment of life as gift (no days to claim, to demand, to expect a right to, to count up as one's own). Insofar as you live in the light of the having been seized, you live without "counting the days." You are not consumed with regret over days past and lost to self-incurvature, or with regret over days never to come due to your own mortality—though in both of these ways you do indeed suffer real loss. But you are not consumed with grief, for your attention is overwhelmingly seized by joy over all Faces, including your own, by delight in all the Faces and wonders of creation, and in the peace of knowing yourself beloved, living having forgiven and having been forgiven.

There is a basis in all of this for real hope and comfort with regard to the final moments of others' lives. Even in cases of relatively sudden death (e.g., automobile accidents, heart attacks, situations such as Effingham's), where one may still experience in full all the shock, terror, and anguish that we imagine accompanies sudden death, we can still hope on behalf of a friend or loved one, indeed, on behalf of all creatures who have died or been killed that, *also*, certainty over their impending and utterly unavoidable death finally broke through all self-incurvature and freed them, with overwhelming purity and intensity, to the redemptive dynamics of that final interval, to the transcending joy of having

---

2. Fyodor Dostoevsky, *The Brothers Karamazov: A Novel in Four Parts with Epilogue*, trans. Richard Pevear and Larissa Volokhonsky (New York: Vintage Classics, 1991), 289.

been seized in and by all the Faces that had filled their life, we can hope that they were gifted for a few final, fleeting but eternally full moments with the surpassing peace of living having forgiven and having been forgiven, and that in their final, fleeting moments they were eternally full of joy and rejoicing for all those Faces who would live on beyond their death.

In other words, we can hope that in their final moments not only those already awakened, but also those whose lives were almost wholly lost to self-incurvature and the logic of domination, that even they were finally broken free from their self-incurvature, and that in their final moments they were awakened and delivered, along with all those who were already living life awakened, into the release of living having forgiven and having been forgiven, into the glory of having been seized in and by love for all Faces, and into delight in all the wonders of creation. In the absence of traumatic physical or psychological impediments, then, one can hope with regard to all creatures, each according to their kind, that in their last moments they were taken up in the paradise of "yes."

There is real, warm comfort here insofar as one can hope that what finally seized and captivated a loved one's or any creature's be-ing in their final moments of eternally full and absolute attention was delight in the Faces and beauty of creation around them and, above all, the glory of having been seized in and by love for all the Faces that filled their lives, the Faces of others long-since dead, and the Faces of all who will live on. We can find some comfort in the thought that, according to his kind, even that gazelle was seized in and by love for all the Faces he had known, that he was overwhelmingly seized into the paradise of "yes" even as the lion's jaws clamped down.

Insofar as you are taken up in the paradise of "yes," death loses its sting, for insofar as life in the paradise of "yes," that is, life lived in the light of having been seized, is life lived having forgiven and having been forgiven, you live in that final interval without bitterness, without accusation, without condemnation, and without self-condemnation. Insofar as life itself is then experienced wholly as gift, your final response-ability in having been seized in and by love is wholly taken up in overwhelming gratitude, delight, and joy. Thus, barring debilitating circumstances, you can face death in that final interval while filled with joy and delight, you can move toward a death that does indeed mark an absolute breaking of relationships and so is something truly to be mourned, but also toward a death that has lost its sting insofar as one is overwhelmingly taken up in and by love for others, overwhelmingly taken up in the paradise of "yes."

MOURNING DEATH

Let me reiterate that even if death in the light of the having been seized loses its sting, it is still rightly mourned. Death still marks what is to all appearances a total loss of self and the absolute end of wonderful relationships. Despite the mitigating joys of the paradise of "yes," death is rightly mourned in relation both to oneself and to others. For instance, if you are about to die and you have young children, you rightly mourn their loss of their mommy or daddy, and you rightly mourn your loss of all those wonderful years nurturing, loving, receiving joy, and taking delight in them as their mother or father. Most of us have felt the burning, irrecoverable absences at weddings, births, recitals, birthdays, graduations, or on Christmas morns. There is no gainsaying such losses, which not even the most literal resurrection and afterlife in heaven could undo. Real-world stories of poignant loss are innumerable. And we do not even begin to deny or look away from the tragic losses of life and of relationships that suffuse reality.

Every death of creatures of every kind should be mourned. Death is not a good to be celebrated or pursued. We should not be interested in suppressing our pain over death in this vale of tears. We should not engage in denial rooted in distracting attacks on God (like Ivan) or in tit-for-tat economies, whether they be religious ("in the long run all is worthwhile because heaven is the pay-off") or matter-of-fact ("suffering and death is the price of happiness and life"). We should not engage in outright denial ("that's just the way it is").

Neither, let me stress, should we depend on appeal to any sort of afterlife, any sort of reincarnation or resurrection of "me" beyond death. Indeed, the idea of life after death can be spiritually dangerous, for it can rob that final interval (i.e., utter acceptance of unavoidable and imminent death) of its potential for bearing a gift for life. For insofar as I am convinced and perhaps even focused on the idea that I will somehow survive my death, the intensity of self-incurvature, that is, the glorification of the atomistic "I" and the drive for I's survival, can be amplified. So there is the very real danger that belief in the reality of life after death will negate the possibility that the near horizon of your own unavoidable death might break or purify you of self-incurvature and open you for the first time or, for those already awakened, open you ever more fully to the glory of the having been seized. In short, belief in life after death, or even (if you cannot quite bring yourself to believe it) a desperate desire to believe in life after death, can bind you all the more tightly to the devastating, self-incurved dynamics of the logic of domination.

Belief in life after death played no part in the awakening, joy, or delight of Markel because belief in life after death plays absolutely no role in the dynamics of the having been seized, plays no role in the dynamics of awakening that can usher us into the paradise of "yes." The dynamics of awakening, the glory of having been seized in and by love for every Face, our wholehearted, if precisely qualified affirmation of reality, of others, and of ourselves, the release of having forgiven and having been forgiven, all of it is concerned and motivated wholly here and now, eyes wide open to all the pain, suffering, and injustice.

To be very clear, with regard to the response to the spiritual challenge of evil unfolded in this book, none of our affirmations, none of our joy, none of our delight, none of our actions, and none of our decisions depend on any belief, expectation, hope, or even any thought of life after death. All the dynamics of awakening, all the dynamics of having been seized in and by love for all Faces including, indirectly but decisively, our own Face, all I have affirmed about the transcending glory of the mutual Face to Face, everything I have affirmed about being released into the peace of having forgiven and having been forgiven, all I have said about the asymmetry and the glory of living in the paradise of the primordial and ultimate "yes": absolutely all of it stands even if, consistent with all appearances, our deaths mark totally, without exception and forevermore, the end of our Faces.

LIFE AFTER DEATH?

While the dynamics of the having been seized and the paradise of "yes" in no way depend on any belief, expectation, or hope in life after death, the question of life after death nonetheless does appropriately and forcefully present itself. The way in which this question arises in the wake of the having been seized is utterly distinct from the way in which this question arises for those who are self-incurved. For the self-incurved, for those lost to the logic of domination, death is an utter disaster, a total negation of everything one's life is ultimately about. So for the self-incurved the question of life after death arises forcefully in terms of concern over one's own death as the paramount and seemingly insurmountable threat to one's ultimate concern: one's own life. In the wake of having been seized in and by love for all Faces, by contrast, the question of life after death arises first and foremost out of love and concern for an innumerable host of particular others.

As we remember the flea, the mother wolf and her pups, the victims of the Indian Ocean tsunami, of the tsunami that struck Japan, of the earthquake that hit Haiti, and as we remember all the children of all species across the ages who have known only brief, brutal lives of loneliness, despair, pain, suffering, and death, it is impossible that the question of the possibility of some life after death, of some second chance for these and a multitude of others, it is impossible that the question of some life after death will not rise up before us *for their sake*, in the form of hope first and foremost *for them*. In terms of sheer hope, for the sake of the suffering multitudes it would be mean-spirited not to at least hope in some sort of literal, good life after death.

This raises a question: Is there any reason for entertaining hope in life, good life, after death? Our answer to this question is incredibly soft for, as noted, the spiritual dangers are terrific, but our answer is positive. First, while there is insufficient basis for belief in life after death, there is by the very nature of the case insufficient basis for belief that there is no life after death, and so we should find the cavalier arrogance with which some modern Westerners dismiss the idea of life after death to be presumptuous. Second, the asymmetry, that is, the primordial and ultimate reality of "yes," taken together with the realization that we are seized in and by love for *particular* Faces, gives us some basis for hoping, *sheerly* hoping, that for each individual, no matter the circumstances of their life and death on earth, there is life after death.[3]

Notably, from the perspective unfolded here, and with particular reference to the asymmetry, it makes sense that over the centuries so many streams among the world's classic wisdom traditions, whether they speak of heaven or the Pure Land, develop a conviction that somehow the reality of the asymmetry, the fact that "yes" is primordial and ultimate, implies that eventually the triumph of the "yes" will somehow be realized totally for every Face. For this same reason, we too can quietly affirm that there is reason for hope—again, sheer hope, not something we conclude, believe, demand, expect, cling to, need, use as a basis for choosing among actions, or utilize in some theodicy or tit-for-tat economy— but reason for hope in some sort of good life after death.

No aspect of this spirituality is in any way dependent on the reality of life after death—this is what I mean when I stress that our hope that there may be life after death is *sheer* hope—however, in the highly qualified and soft sense just specified, the dynamics of this philosophical spirituality do give reason for sheer hope that there is good life after death, and most especially for sheer hope that the story is not over for all those others who lived lives brutal and brief.[4]

Let me be clear, however, about the heart of this philosophical spirituality and stress that for its understanding of the paradise of "yes," no belief, expectation, hope, or even thought of life after death is essential, for the core reality at the heart of our understanding, the paramount "fact that matters," the reality over which, once we are awakened, we cannot help but have complete and joyous surety, is the reality of agape. This core reality, this reality that is primordial and ultimate (alpha and omega), this transcending reality in which we live and move and have our being, is the reality of having been seized in and by love for all Faces, including our own.

This is the divine reality, the reality of agape, the reality of a transcending, amazing grace in which we live and move and have our being. This is the reality of the God who is love, the reality that—even as our eyes remain wide open to evil, even as we unreservedly confess our complicity and culpability, and even as we do not fail to notice and do not fail to act in response to concrete threats to Faces—this is the divine reality that delivers us unto the glory of having forgiven all others and of having been forgiven ourselves. This is the reality that frees us to innocent delight in eros, and to the joy "made complete" of mutually awakened, Face-to-Face communion, the joy of koinonia. This is the saving reality that allows us to transcend the threefold spiritual challenge of affirmation in the face of enduring evil and to live in the light of a primordial and ultimate "yes" to

3. The insistence on the primordial and ultimate worth of *each* Face may mark the root distinction between monotheistic and monistic spiritualities.

4. A complementary reflection on life after death can be found in William Greenway, *A Reasonable Belief: Why God and Faith Make Sense* (Louisville, KY: Westminster John Knox Press, 2015), 147–49.

reality, to others, and to ourselves. For, as this wholly reasonable exploration in philosophical spirituality allows us to testify—insofar as we do not harden our hearts, insofar as we are awakened and live surrender to the gift of agape—we live in the glorious light of amazing grace.

Afterword

Philosophical Spirituality and Christian Theology

Even where familiarity does not breed contempt, it can dull discernment and short-circuit appreciation. Precisely because the *Mona Lisa* is so familiar, for instance, it can be difficult to appreciate the qualities that made it celebrated in the first place. The same can be true for those raised as Christians with regard to familiar Scriptures and common theological terms. That is one reason I have largely avoided familiar theological terms and Scripture throughout this exploration.

The second reason I have largely avoided familiar terms is to guard against surreptitious dependence on special revelation. To be clear, this is not to reject the legitimacy of special revelation. However, since this is a philosophical spirituality, an exploration wholly within the bounds of what is generally considered reasonable and good (spirituality within the limits of reason alone, one might say), it is important to guard against surreptitious dependence on special revelation.

While I have proceeded within the bounds of what is generally accepted to be reasonable and good, it is not humanly possible to speak from some transcendent "view from nowhere" or "God's-eye view." I am a male, second-generation Italian/Scotch-English American, middle class (my grandparents were economic immigrants), modern Western Christian theologian and philosopher. On the other hand, acknowledgment of contextual specificity does not entail affirmation of wholesale relativity or warrant irrational appeals. For while all human understanding and truth claims are relative to cultural context and the potentials of some language or another, the realities that human understanding and truth claims *are about*—for instance, the realities signified by the word "agape" or the word "gravity"— are not relative.

Insofar as diverse cultures and faith traditions are truly dealing with a transcending reality, it is reasonable to expect all faiths have been inspired by and developed in response to the same transcending reality, the reality the Christian tradition speaks of in terms of agape. As a Christian, I cannot speak definitively for other faith traditions. At the same time, since it is reasonable to expect that all faith traditions have been developed in response to the same transcending reality, it is reasonable to expect the essence of Christian spirituality to be continuous with the essence of Jewish, Islamic, Hindu, and Buddhist spiritualities (among others). If so, then I would expect my Christian exploration of faith, and my quintessentially Christian understanding of the way in which agape gifts us with faith that delivers affirmation without evasion of evil, to be in essential spiritual accord with other faith traditions. Insofar as that is the case, this unfolding of the reality and far-reaching, saving power of agape is globally relevant, is an unveiling of a single, transcending, universal reality—though the ways in which that same reality and its significance are described in various faith traditions may vary.

Because I have been striving to address the spiritual challenge of evil within the boundaries of general revelation, the connections between this philosophical spirituality and distinctly Christian theology, though ubiquitous, have remained largely oblique (though hopefully not obscure). In this afterword, still remaining within the bounds of general revelation, I want very briefly to make some explicit connections to Christian theology.

I began this exploration by unfolding the spiritual challenge of affirmation in the face of evil: namely, by making clear our inability, once we step beyond various forms of denial, to affirm the world, others, and ourselves. I described the depths of the spiritual challenge of evil in terms of a world suffused with pain, suffering, and injustice, a world that is structured so that everywhere life and flourishing is parasitic on destruction, death, and predation. Christians call this the "fallenness" of the world. The "fall" in this theological sense does not designate a temporal, historical event. The "fall" is not something that happened in time as a consequence of human actions. "Fallen" names how we discern this world of pain, suffering, and injustice in the light of having been seized in and by love for all Faces. To describe the world as fallen, then, is to name squarely all the evil suffusing reality and to acknowledge that we cannot affirm the world.

I also pointed out that from our first glimmerings of self-awareness we find ourselves already thrown into this fallen reality. This is a reality from which we do not stand apart in splendid, innocent isolation. This is the reality from which we first emerge and of which we are wholly a part. Thereby this is a reality with which we are always already complicit—through our very existing, before any intention or action on our part. Christians speak of this, our emergence and existence part and parcel of this fallen world, in terms of *original sin*. Original sin, like the fall, does not designate a temporal, historical event or action or its consequences. "Original sin" designates how we who are awakened discern the complicity of every creature, each of which exists part and parcel of this vale of tears. To describe ourselves and others as guilty of original sin, then, is to acknowledge that we are part of this fallen world.

Though I focused on the fallen character of the world and original sin, not even saints deny their intentional, willful culpability, that is, not even saints deny culpability where, through action or inaction, they have wounded Faces. In other words, with regard to others and to ourselves, there are two dimensions to our guilt. We are not only "original sinners/complicit" but also "personal sinners/culpable." In sum, then, insofar as we are not only complicit but also culpable in a fallen world, and insofar as we do not harden our hearts (deny or evade the reality of evil), we are unable straightforwardly to affirm this world, others, or ourselves. Therefore, I argued, we are confronted with the spiritual challenge of evil or, more precisely, with the spiritual, threefold challenge of affirmation in the face of evil.[1]

The apostle Paul's formulation of the stakes of the spiritual challenge of affirmation in the New Testament is especially potent: the wages of sin is death. Insofar as personal survival is usually a paramount concern, it is easy to think Paul is speaking primarily about biological death. No doubt Paul and mainstream Christianity have had biological death in mind, and resurrection to eternal life was also thought of in terms of resurrection to life after death. Nothing I am saying counts against this dimension of Paul's meaning or counts against the possibility of life after death (though it appears this would take us beyond the bounds of a philosophical spirituality). But even if there is literal life after death, biological death is not Paul's emphasis where the wages of sin are concerned, and while eternal life may also refer to life after death, in the New Testament eternal life is first and foremost a *present* possibility, a distinctive way of being in the world.

Above all, Paul is focused on spiritual dimensions of existence, on spiritual life and the spiritual consequences of sin. The "death" that is the wages of sin is first and foremost spiritual death, not biological death. The spiritual death that is the wages of sin is first and foremost life overcome by guilt, wherein one is unable to meet the spiritual challenge of evil, wherein one is forced finally to conclude

---

1. Notably, in some modern streams of Christian theology it has become common to dismiss the doctrines of the fall and of original sin. Some have even attacked these doctrines for being naive and oppressive. From the perspective of this philosophical spirituality, affirmation of the reality of the pain, suffering, and injustice suffusing reality (i.e., the truth of the fall) and of the complicity of every being whose existence trades on this fallen reality (i.e., the truth of original sin) is simply a matter of honesty ("facing up," one might say) with regard to obvious truths about reality.

concerning life in this world, including one's own life: "*it's no good.*" The gift of God, accordingly, is grace, the forgiveness of sins, salvation from judgment, deliverance from guilt. Insofar as we do not harden our hearts, insofar as we live surrender to having been seized in and by love for all Faces, that is, insofar as we live by faith, the gift of grace, we are saved from living condemnation, from living death, which is the wages of sin, and delivered unto living "yes," unto living, right now, eternal life.

In other words, unsurprisingly, the core focus of the New Testament witness is spiritual. Above all, it proclaims spiritual salvation from spiritual affliction. Spiritual salvation to eternal life—that is, living eternally *right now*—is salvation to primordial and ultimate affirmation of the world, others, and ourselves. Spiritual salvation to eternal life is freedom from lives of guilt and condemnation, salvation from lives consumed in futile denial of the reality of evil, salvation from devastatingly confused hardening of our hearts, salvation to the reality of having been seized in and by love for all Faces, including our own. Salvation to eternal life is salvation to life lived in surrender to the glorious light of having been seized in and by love. In classic terms, it is salvation realized in living faith that is the gift of grace (*sola gratia, sola fide*).

Of course, we live with enduring evil, with enduring complicity and culpability. With recognition of the decisive asymmetry, however, we understand that while evil is real it is derivative, for it names "yes-violated." Acknowledging without any evasion or denial the full horror of evil does not mark the defeat of "yes," does not undo having been seized in and by love. To the contrary, at its worst evil marks the intensification of our passion and conviction over the truth of the having been seized, which often reaches its highest inflection in terrible contexts, where it generates our screamed and horrified "*No!*"

The spiritual power of agape is not a physical power, not a power that in and of itself could stop a Hitler or prevent the cancer (though, to be sure, it is the spiritual reality of agape that fires physical and sociopolitical struggle against evil). While we are not talking about physical power, however, we are speaking to the most significant power of all, the only power, for instance, that can lead you willingly to give up your life (i.e., out of love), the power that can bring incomparable spiritual joy and peace or, over and against its violation, the power that can yield incomparable horror and sorrow, the power whose significance can dwarf the significance of physical pleasure or pain, the power that can deliver us to a primordial and ultimate "yes" to the world, to others, and to ourselves, the power of God insofar as God is love.

Notably, while physical powers are terrifically significant, and can kill the most faithful Faces, with regard to the spiritual challenge of affirmation in the face of evil, all physical powers (even the physical powers of a divine agent) are impotent. Moreover, the primordial and ultimate meaningfulness of all physical powers is indexed to their spiritual significance, to their good or ill for Faces. While spiritual power is physically helpless against physical power, then, physical powers are spiritually impotent, and the meaningfulness of physical powers, to good or ill, is dependent on spiritual power. For those who are awakened, agape not only determines all judgment (so, for instance, we name all the pain, suffering, and injustice as evil) but also inspires good and wise action in the world (i.e., physical, sociocultural action).

In this spiritual sense we can speak with rich moral contour about God as the source, ground, and end (*telos*) of all spiritual significance, we can concretely characterize in terms of agape our utter and absolute dependence on this spiritual power, all of which is a way of declaring this power, the power of gracious love, the power of agape, the power of God, to be primordial and ultimate, eternal. We could perhaps even speak in this carefully qualified, nonanthropomorphic sense of God's omniscience and omnipotence.

I have unfolded "God" in terms of a classic Christian, biblical confession: "God *is* love/agape." When I talk about agape being "primordial and ultimate," I am using different terms to designate what in the Bible is spoken of in terms of God being "alpha and omega." "Primordial and ultimate" is also closely related to the theological idea of God as "eternal," which is not a temporal category, but a gesture to a reality that transcends time, space, and all other empirical reality (i.e., "eternal" is not "everlasting"—a temporal category—but "outside or apart from time").

While "primordial and ultimate," "alpha and omega," "eternal" and "transcendent" sound like distant realities, insofar as God is known in the reality of having been seized and by love for all Faces, including our own, insofar as God is the reality at the heart of our "*Yes*'s" and our "*No*'s," the source of all our moral responsiveness, conviction, and affirmation, then God is also the most immediate, significant, and intimate reality in our lives. I unfolded the character of God's significance with classic theological terms and meaning, namely, in terms of grace, forgiveness, and confession, and with an urgent caution not to harden one's heart, but to surrender to having been seized in and by the gracious love of God.

Notably, the "always already" character of the having been seized, in other words, its eternal character, its standing as a transcending reality that first seizes us, is identified in classic Christian theology with the specification that grace/agape is *prevenient*. In common Christian testimony, this priority of the divine is expressed in phrases such as, "I did not find God, I found myself found," "knew myself known," "found myself already fully known and accepted," "was filled with joy as I realized that before I knew God, God already knew and loved me."

My neo-Levinasian specification of the relation between the transcending agape that first seizes us and autonomy, namely, our capacity to harden our hearts to having been seized in and by love for Faces, explains how faith, which flows to us insofar as we do not harden our hearts, is dependent on our autonomy/choice while not being a product of our autonomy/choice. In other words, my description of faith as the saving gift of grace that is ours insofar as we do not harden our hearts explains how faith can be both ours and at the same time not one of our works. Of course, insofar as we do not harden our hearts, insofar as we are faithful, we immediately and passionately engage in works out of fidelity to the Faces by which we have been seized (or, theologians might say, the specific Faces that, through our having been seized in and by love, have elected us). But faith saves, not works—though passion for good works is an immediate fruit of faith ("faith without works is dead" or "you will know them by their fruits").

My talk (following Levinas) about "Faces," meanwhile, covers all that is essential in traditional theological talk of "souls," but without suggesting any sort of ghostly, not-quite-material-but-still-somehow-thingly-stuff-that-is-what-we-really-are, a ghostly stuff that is mysteriously attached to our bodies and free-floats somewhere after our deaths. Precisely as all creatures, even dogs, cats, and saplings have Faces, so all creatures have souls. In contrast to a widespread and sterile modern Western vision of existence, which tends to divide reality between humans and the world/environment, and perhaps also to imagine a God who is radically elsewhere, this neo-Levinasian vision is in far greater accord with the reach and intimacy of the biblical vision, which sees humans as a kind of creature living among diverse kinds of creatures, all living in creation in intimate communion with an eternal, gracious Creator.

I would argue that my neo-Levinasian unfolding of the dynamics of agape and forgiveness has even captured the essence of the Christian notion of substitutionary atonement—though admittedly not in a common sense. Many Christians understand substitutionary atonement in a transactional sense. That is, they understand atonement wholly within the closed, tit-for-tat (or "economic") terms of the sphere of justice. For example, on one influential account sin is understood to create a debt that must be paid in turn. On this account, God in one way or another pays a debt or ransom for us—in the bloodiest versions the debt or ransom is somehow paid, or the honor redeemed (there are multiple variations), through Jesus' blood and death on the cross.

How suffering undoes any offense or, even more bizarre, how the unjust suffering and death of an innocent person undoes any offense (instead of magnifying the degree of injustice and so exacerbating the problem), or how God's oft-reputed move to have an innocent punished in order to pay the penalty for the sin of the guilty could in itself be a just decision (who in the world thinks punishing the innocent for the guilty is a good and just thing to do?) all remains unexplained. Worse yet, there is no obvious role for grace in transactional (tit-for-tat) atonement theories.[2] Indeed, the possibility of

---

2. To gesture toward the *reductio ad absurdum* I would develop in terms of transactional theories of atonement (e.g., penal substitutionary atonement theories), in the end (using the traditional language) they need to explain *why* God would decide to sacrifice God's only begotten, wholly innocent Son (even if understood in terms of God's self-sacrifice) so that those who are truly guilty can be freed of all culpability and treated as if they are wholly innocent. In terms of justice, there is no justification for such a decision, no reason ever to make the move. In order to explain that move, transactional theories of atonement will need to abandon the sphere of justice and make an appeal to God's grace—at which point the demand for an explanation in terms of justice, which lies at the heart of transactional theories in the first place, is rendered moot (in a word, transactional theories confusedly demand an explanation for grace be given using the incommensurable categories of justice). On the other hand, I would want to remember that transactional theories of atonement,

grace playing the decisive, or any, role, is elided in all transactional atonement theories, for all remain within the tit-for-tat sphere of justice (where to forgive without recompense is considered to be unjust, for the offense is understood to create a debt or ransom that must somehow be repaid).

Substitution on the neo-Levinasian understanding I am suggesting here, by contrast, pivots wholly on grace, that is, on the primordial and ultimate, eternal power of agape. In accord with the testimony of generations of Christians, the substitution that immediately yields forgiveness and release into the paradise of "yes" happens with surrender to having been seized in and by love for all Faces, including my own. What the power of agape replaces is my own striving, my attempts to ground and establish myself, my attempts, in a word, to save myself. What is substituted for my own striving, a substitution realized when I abandon all grasping, all struggle to stand on my own two feet (i.e., all struggle for radical autonomy) is the primordial and ultimate power of agape/grace/God manifest in the having been seized. This substitution describes the dynamics of the life of faith, life lived in surrender to having been seized in and by love, life lived having forgiven and having been forgiven, life lived in the paradise of "yes."[3]

I am only gesturing in these closing pages to the relationship between this philosophical spirituality and specifically Christian theology. By this point I hope it is clear that the spiritual challenge of evil is not a secondary theological motif but addresses the heart of Christian theology, the very essence of Christian understanding of a supreme spiritual challenge, and the very essence of Christian understanding of salvation and faith that is the gift of grace. Let me close this entire exploration by unfolding this claim in conversation with a familiar Gospel story about Jesus, namely, the story of Jesus healing a man with paralysis, a man who has been lowered through an earthen roof by loyal friends (Mark 2:1–12, Luke 5:17–26).

In this story Jesus is teaching a tightly bunched group of people inside a fairly large house. Four men arrive outside the house carrying a friend, who is paralyzed, on a mat. Unable to get into the house, the intrepid friends dig through the roof and lower their friend before Jesus. If one can imagine odd sounds giving way to a hole emerging in the ceiling, and then a man being lowered to the floor in front of Jesus, one can readily imagine that the friends succeeded in capturing the attention of Jesus and everyone else! If I can make my point in playful but still serious fashion, this Scripture has great comic potential.

To play out my comic take on the passage, I need a dry, sardonic lead, so I put Bill Murray in the role of the man with paralysis. He's lying on a cot, paralyzed

even if they are theoretically confused, possibly gained currency because they met important pastoral/psychological needs to which we should remain attentive (see especially on this point Cynthia Rigby, "Are You Saved? Receiving the Full Benefits of Grace," *Insights* 115:2 [Spring 2000]: 3–18).

3. This is the character of the saving faith of Jesus Christ and of Abraham that Paul is talking about in Romans 3 and 4. Along the same lines, when Paul speaks of the "righteousness" of God he is speaking not of the *justice* of God but of the primordial and ultimate *agape/grace* of God, the agape that is simultaneously the root of God's derivative/penultimate but nonetheless passionate concern over injustice (i.e., violation of agape).

from the waist down. Bill Murray clings to the sides of the cot as his determined friends struggle to get him up onto the roof, and again after they cut a hole in the roof and lower him down in front of Jesus. A high camera angle from the back of the room shows the shadowed heads of the crowd in the foreground, beyond them the sun puts a natural spotlight on Murray and Jesus. Then the picture changes and we are focused on Jesus. Jesus looks down at Murray, says, "Your sins are forgiven," and then continues teaching the crowd. We quickly cut to a shot of an incredulous Murray, who, with an almost imperceptible nod towards his legs, looks up at Jesus and says in his famous deadpan, "um, that's not why I'm here" (cue laugh track).

Of course, the man with paralysis says no such thing. But we are concerned with being paralyzed, or being blind, or ill, or with death, so it is easy for us to hear or remember this passage and think that the really significant thing Jesus did for the man was heal him of his paralysis. But this is not what the Scripture says. Jesus looks down at the man and says, "your sins are forgiven"— and immediately moves on. When Jesus does eventually heal the man from paralysis, he does not heal the man for the man's sake, but for the sake of the Pharisees. The point, of course, is not that Jesus did not really care for the man; the point is that Jesus addressed the paramount need, the spiritual need. Jesus named a spiritual healing the man had received that was so profound that the paralysis was literally unremarkable. "Your sins are forgiven." What is the disease that so afflicts us, or *should* so afflict us that—once we move beyond all denial, all evasion, all hardening of our hearts—by comparison being paralyzed is not worth mention?

It is significant that in fact the man with paralysis does not give the comic response I imagined. His silent reception of Jesus' gift signals that this man has profound spiritual discernment of his most profound affliction. He is evidently spiritually awakened and discerning enough to recognize that the most significant miracle, the most profound gift he has been given, is salvation from sin, peace that passes understanding, deliverance unto the paradise of yes.

Affirmation of the literal healing of the man's paralysis, which Jesus eventually does for the sake of skeptics, appears to lie beyond the bounds of philosophical spirituality, but in the final analysis that is of little consequence, for our philosophical spirituality can discern and confidently affirm the most significant gift, the spiritual gift, the awakening to having been seized in and by love delivered in the encounter with Jesus, the realization of the forgiveness of sins, the deliverance into the paradise of yes.

It is easy to misinterpret this passage because our concerns are easily misplaced. We tend to prioritize physical realities and as a result we lose sight of the significance of spiritual realities. This dynamic is amplified with regard to physical life and death. When physical life and death stakes are in play, it is especially easy to lose sight of spiritual realities and to think of "eternal life" primarily in physical terms, that is, in terms of resurrection to life after death. In the New Testament, however, eternal life does not typically refer to everlasting life, eternal life is not primarily a reference to life after death. Eternal life in the New Testament is almost always an immediately present and continuing reality. Jesus repeatedly called people to turn and be saved, *right then*, just as he calls on us to turn and live eternal life, *right now*. Eternal life is not primarily future life after death. Eternal life is first and foremost a way of living here and now.

The spiritual challenge of evil is not a special or secondary topic in theology. In naming our complicity and culpability in a fallen world and discerning a way through to primordial and ultimate affirmation of creation, all others, and ourselves, I am unfolding the spiritual challenge and the spiritual salvation at the heart of the gospel of Jesus.

The dynamics I am identifying here are consistent with classic Christian testimony. Consider the testimony of John Newton, testimony immortalized in his beloved, spiritually profound hymn, "Amazing Grace." John Newton captained a slave ship—a brutal paradigm for evil in this world. Many people are familiar with the first and fifth verses of "Amazing Grace." The first: "Amazing grace, how sweet the sound, that saved a wretch like me! I once was lost, but now am found, was blind, but now I see."[4] And the last: "When we've been there ten thousand years, bright shining as the sun, we've no less days to sing God's praise than when we'd first begun." Notably, Newton did not write that last stanza, which so dangerously tempts us to see physical death as the real enemy, which so dangerously directs our attention away from this world and away from the realized, saving, this-worldly grace Newton testifies to with such passion and discernment.

"'Twas grace that taught my heart to fear, and grace my fears relieved. How precious did that grace appear the hour I first believed!" Here Newton testifies with beauty and brevity to the essential, saving spiritual paradox of the gospel message, which is also the essential, saving spiritual paradox at the heart of the testimony of this philosophical spirituality: awakening to having been seized in and by love for every Face is awakening to all the pain, suffering, and injustice suffusing this vale of tears (i.e., awakening to "yes" is awakening to "yes-violated"), and so it is awakening to my own complicity and culpability. However, since this awakening is primordial and ultimate awakening to gracious love, a love that is wholly given to us despite our complicity and culpability, no matter how awful, this grace both teaches our hearts to fear and delivers us from those fears, both awakens us to the spiritual challenge of evil and simultaneously delivers us unto the paradise of yes.

Newton, like the man with paralysis, understands. Death is not his ultimate enemy. He knows already he is not really living. He knows, given all the blood and horror on his hands, that he has no hope of ever saving or affirming himself. He feels the crushing reality of the threefold challenge of affirmation in the face of evil. His complicity and culpability with the brutal reality, his inability to

---

4. John Newton, "Amazing Grace," in *Glory to God* (Louisville, KY: Westminster John Knox Press, 2013), 649.

affirm the world, others, and himself, was driven home with utter clarity. Then, utterly beyond what he deserved and beyond what he could possibly hope for, he stops resisting and surrenders utterly to having been seized in and by agape. Immediately he is seized by a firm and certain knowledge of God's benevolence toward him, and he begins to live eternally, to live forgiven.

"The Lord has promised good to me; his word my hope secures. He will my shield and portion be as long as life endures." As the final phrase—"as long as life endures"—makes clear, for Newton the Lord's shield is not a shield against death, and the promised good is not life after death. The hope secured is hope for eternal living *now*, a shield against condemnation even as we continue to live alive to our enduring complicity and culpability. The good is forgiveness of sins and affirmation, amazing grace, God's peace, peace that transcends understanding.

This does not mean that Newton did not believe in literal life after death, a traditional Christian hope, nor am I rejecting that possibility, though positive affirmation appears to lie beyond the bounds of a philosophical spirituality. But the issue of life after death is neither his focus nor the central gift of Christian faith. Life in heaven would be wonderful, like being healed of paralysis, but it is not *the* thing, it does not speak to the essence of Christian hope and joy. Moreover, I do not have any claim on life after death, as if I can demand more, deserve more, as if in the end I have been wronged if I do not get to live forever. Physical death is to be avoided (usually) and mourned, for it does cut life short and, even if there is life after death, it does cut us off from wonderful relationships. Nonetheless, it is not our most devastating enemy. Living death, the death that is the wages of sin, the death that cuts us off from eternal living of however many days we are given in this world, that death is our most devastating enemy. It is that living death that is defeated by grace, the grace that delivers us unto eternal life right now, the gift that secures our good for as long as life endures.

Given the reality and conviction that grace is primordial and ultimate, it is, to say again, not unreasonable to hope that somehow, beyond our comprehension, there ultimately will be a literal and complete restoration of all creatures, a new heavens and a new earth, some sort of literal heaven. Again, it would be cruel not at least to hope for some sort of literal life after death on behalf of all those creatures whose lives have been brutal and short. But literal life after death is neither essential nor the point. On this we find agreement even in Gospel narratives about the resurrected Jesus.

In Luke 24, for instance, when Jesus appears to his disciples after his crucifixion and burial, his first words are, "Peace be with you" (v.36). He goes on to say the message to be preached to all nations in his name as a result of his death and resurrection is "repentance and the forgiveness of sins" (v. 47). Not, "look, death is defeated" and "you too will get to live again after you die," but this: "peace be with you" and "repentance and forgiveness of sins." Here, as with the story of the healing of the man with paralysis, a philosophical spirituality is able to discern the most significant reality and promise, the spiritual reality and promise. Philosophical spirituality is able to affirm and proclaim the heart of the gospel of Jesus, which speaks first and foremost to salvation from the wages of sin, to salvation from the living death that is life in this world lived apart from the glorious, saving light of having been seized in and by love.

Just as with literal healing of paralysis, literal resurrection to life after death stands beyond the bounds of a philosophical spirituality. A philosophical spirituality, however, is able to discern, affirm, and proclaim the essential and most significant point: peace, blessed peace, the peace of God, the peace that transcends understanding, the peace that comes with repentance and the forgiveness of sins, the peace of Jesus' own, "peace be with you."

There is much more to say about the relationship between a philosophical spirituality and distinctively Christian theology, but already one can see how the point of the life, ministry, suffering, and death of Jesus, and even resurrection to new life, has to do above all with "repentance and the forgiveness of sins," with living eternally here and now, with a peace given to us here and now in the flesh. Awakened to this amazing love for all Faces, we are moved to proclaim forgiveness of sins to all peoples and to urge total, unmitigated repentance (". . . guilty . . . I most of all . . .").

Having been seized in and by love for all Faces, we offer our testimony in the hope that all people may be awakened and find themselves asking in joyful amazement with Markel, "am I not in paradise now?" Having been seized in and by love for the diverse host of concrete Faces that elect each of us day by day, we are immediately moved to celebrate and support their flourishing, or to mourn and act to give aid or provide resistance if they are suffering or oppressed.

Finally, with regard to the spiritual challenge of evil, inspired by agape, living by faith, that is, living surrender to the having been seized, we offer up our testimony in the hope that everyone, eyes wide open to all the pain, suffering, and injustice suffusing reality, that is, eyes wide open to evil, and wholly confessing enduring complicity and culpability, may nevertheless rejoice and sing with John Newton, "Amazing grace, how sweet the sound, that saved a wretch like me! I once was lost, but now am found, was blind but now I see."

Bibliography

Allen, Diogenes. *The Path of Perfect Love*. Cambridge: Cowley Publications, 1992.

Burtt, E. A. *The Metaphysical Foundations of Modern Science*. Revised Edition. Amherst, NY: Humanity Books, 1999.

Callicott, J. Baird. *Beyond the Land Ethic: More Essays in Environmental Philosophy*. New York: SUNY Press, 1999.

The Cambridge Companion to Levinas. Edited by Simon Critchley and Robert Bernasconi. Cambridge: Cambridge University Press, 2002.

Chamberlain, Lesley. *Nietzsche in Turin: An Intimate Biography*. New York: Picador USA, 1999.

Deep Ecology for the 21st Century: Readings on the Philosophy and Practice of the New Environmentalism. Edited by George Sessions. Boston: Shambhala Publications, Inc., 1995.

Dostoevsky, Fyodor. *The Brothers Karamazov: A Novel in Four Parts with Epilogue*. Translated by Richard Pevear and Larissa Volokhonsky. New York: Vintage Classics, 1991.

Dreyfus, Hubert and Charles Taylor. *Retrieving Realism*. Boston: Harvard University Press, 2015.

Glory to God. Louisville, KY: Westminster John Knox Press, 2013.

Greenway, William. "Charles Taylor on Affirmation, Mutilation, and Theism: A Retrospective Reading of *Sources of the Self*." *Journal of Religion* 80 (January 2000): 23–40.

_____. *For the Love of All Creatures: The Story of Grace in Genesis*. Grand Rapids: William B. Eerdmans Publishing Co., 2015.

_____. "Peter Singer, Emmanuel Levinas, Christian Agape, and the Spiritual Heart of Animal Liberation." *Journal of Animal Ethics* 5:2 (Fall 2015): 167–80.

_____. *A Reasonable Belief: Why God and Faith Make Sense*. Louisville, KY: Westminster John Knox Press, 2015.

Hamburger, Michael. "Rilke among the Critics." *Encounter* 103 (April, 1962): 46–51.

Hartshorne, Charles. *Born to Sing: An Interpretation and World Survey of Bird Song*. Bloomington: Indiana University Press, 1992.

Heidegger, Martin. *Being and Time*. Translated by Joan Stambaugh. Revised by Dennis Schmidt. Albany: State University of New York Press, 2010.

Leopold, Aldo. *A Sand County Almanac.* New York: Oxford University Press, 1987.

Levinas, Emmanuel. *Difficult Freedom: Essays on Judaism.* Translated by Seán Hand. Baltimore: The John Hopkins University Press, 1997.

_____. *Entre Nous: Thinking-of-the-Other.* Translated by Michael Smith and Barbara Harshav. New York: Columbia University Press, 1998.

_____. *Is It Righteous to Be? Interviews with Emmanuel Levinas.* Edited by Jill Robbins. Stanford, CA: Stanford University Press, 2001.

_____. *Otherwise Than Being, or Beyond Essence.* Translated by Alphonso Lingis. Pittsburgh: Duquesne University Press, 1981.

_____. "The Paradox of Morality: an Interview with Emmanuel Levinas." Translated by Andrew Benjamin and Tamra Wright. In *The Provocation of Levinas: Rethinking the other.* Edited by Robert Bernasconi and David Wood. London: Routledge, 1988: 168–80.

Marion, Jean-Luc. "Sketch of a Phenomenological Concept of Gift." In *Postmodern Philosophy and Christian Thought.* Edited by Merold Westphal. Bloomington: Indiana University Press, 1999.

Malka, Salomon. *Emmanuel Levinas: His Life and Legacy.* Translated by Michael Kigel and Sonja M. Embree. Pittsburgh: Duquesne University Press, 2006.

Murdoch, Iris. *Metaphysics as a Guide to Morals.* New York: Penguin Books, 1993.

_____. *The Unicorn.* London: Penguin Books, 1963.

Naess, Arne. "Self-Realization: An Ecological Approach to Being in the World." In *Thinking Like a Mountain: Towards a Council of All Beings.* Edited by John Seed, Joanna Macy, Pat Fleming, and Arne Naess. Philadelphia: New Society Publishers, 1988.

Nietzsche, Friedrich. *The Anti-Christ, Ecce Homo, Twilight of the Idols, and Other Writings.* Translated by A. Judith Norman. Edited by Aaron Ridley. Cambridge: Cambridge University Press, 2005.

Pascal, Blaise. *Pensées.* Translated by A. J. Krailsheimer. New York: Penguin Books, 1966.

Pevear, Richard. "Introduction." In *The Brothers Karamazov: A Novel in Four Parts with Epilogue*, by Fyodor Dostoevsky. Translated by Richard Pevear and Larissa Volokhonsky. New York: Vintage Classics, 1991.

Rigby, Cynthia. "Are You Saved? Receiving the Full Benefits of Grace." *Insights* 115:2 (Spring 2000): 3–18.

Russell, Bertrand. "The Free Man's Worship." In *The Collected Papers of Bertrand Russell, v. 12: Contemplation and Action, 1902–1914.* Edited by Richard A. Rempel, Andrew Brink, and Margaret Moran. London: George Allen & Unwin, 1985.

Shakespeare, William. *Macbeth.*

Spender, Stephen. *The Struggle of the Modern.* Berkeley: University of California Press, 1963.

Stevens, Wallace. *Opus Posthumous.* New York: Alfred A. Knopf, 1957.

Taylor, Charles. *The Ethics of Authenticity.* Boston: Harvard University Press, 1992.

_____. *Philosophical Arguments.* Boston: Harvard University Press, 1997.

_____. *A Secular Age.* Boston: Harvard University Press, 2007.

_____. *Sources of the Self: The Making of the Modern Identity.* Cambridge: Harvard University Press, 1989.

Thoreau, Henry David. *Walking.* Rockville, MD: Arc Manor, 2007.

Index of Names

CPSIA information can be obtained
at www.ICGtesting.com
Printed in the USA
FFOW04n1233281016
28857FF